sixty-seven poems for downtrodden saints

Jack

Micheline

sixty-
seven
poems
for
downtrodden
saints

FMSBW • San Francisco • 1999

Copyright © 1997 by Jack Micheline
Copyright © 1999 by Vincent Silvaer
All Rights Reserved

Edited by Matt Gonzalez
Cover photo by Ramon Muxter
Frontispiece drawing by Eddie Balchowsky
Graphic production by Joseph Stubbs & Kurt Bigenho

All drawings and paintings reproduced in the text are by Jack Micheline and appear courtesy of Matt Gonzalez, except the painting *Arthur Rimbaud*, which appears courtesy of Billy Childish.

Published by:
FMSBW
84 Sycamore Street
San Francisco, CA 94110

Distributed by:
The Jack Micheline Foundation for the Arts
P.O. Box 30153
Tucson, AZ 85751
http://www.jackmicheline.com

First edition, June 1997.
100 copies hardbound of which 67 are numbered and signed, 26 are lettered A to Z and signed with an original drawing and handwritten poem by the author, and 7 are inscribed as gifts to women poets respected and admired by the author. 300 copies softbound.

Second edition revised, January 1999.
1,500 copies hardbound of which 100 include a tipped-in gouache painting by the author and are numbered and signed by the author's son Vincent Silvaer and the editor Matt Gonzalez.

ISBN 0–9666696–0–6

Contents

Biographical Note   i
Mr Jack Micheline   x
Bibliography   xi

Poem: crooked streets   3
Long Corridor   4
Beauty Is Everywhere Baudelaire   6
Hiding Places   8
It Is Dusk   11
Down by the Wild   12
My Head   14
Poem: I am a poet   16
Poet of the Streets   19
Under the Stands   22
All People Are Enslaved   24
Poem to the Freaks   26
Poem to a Dead Pigeon   28
Long After Midnight   31
B Train   34
On Columbia Heights   35
Statement on Poetry   37
The Dead Are Gone   38
My City   39
To the Always Hunted   43
Everywhere I Go   45

Poem: I chose the whippoorwill	47
A Song to Celebrate Life	48
To Be a Poet Is to Live and Die	50
These Streets I Walk Upon	53
Poem to Apollinaire	56
For Genet	58
Poems Are for Sissies	60
To My Grandfather	62
Poem: I kiss the dead face of a Russian girl	63
Poem to Fernando and the Sky over Paris	64
The Indigent Soul	66
Poem Written on a Hollywood Back Street Sunday Morning	68
On Franz Kline	72
My University of Learning	74
Green	75
Illumination	78
Night City	80
Sainthood Is for the Birds	83
In the Depths	86
Poem: The soul weeps	87
Warren Finnerty Riding a Bicycle on 4th Avenue at Midnight Dreaming of Love and Wine and Franz Kline	89
Stone of the Heart	92
Blues Poem	94
Poem to Buk and the Brave	97
Let's Sing a Song	105

One Arm	109
Poem to the Seventeenth of November 1962	110
This My Friend Is How Rare Poems Are Written	112
Rambling Jack	115
Old Maid (a song)	120
Prologue to East Bleeker	122
Someday I'll Live Forever	125
A Real Poem	127
These Cities	128
Streetcall New Orleans	129
South Street Pier	134
Poem to Bob Kaufman	136
Chasing Kerouac's Shadow	139
Poem on a Drunken Evening	145
Praise to the Original Mind Who Breathes Fresh Air	146
Red Haired Goddess	151
Fragment	152
Shuffling the Deck	154
Black Day in Spain	157
The Ballad of Jimmy Nelson	158
2nd Avenue Discount	160
The Streets Are Yours Bobby Bolles	161
Blues for a Blonde	162
Prologue to My Reading	163
Jenny Lee	165
Back of Town Blues	167

Eternity	169
A Poet Can Be a Shoemaker	171
Requiem	172
Beauford Delaney in Paris 1964	174
Untitled	176
Souls	179
Make Your Color in the Sky	189
Personal	191
Poem: To capture the feeling	193
I Wink at the Graveyards in Queens	197
Bowery Black	198
Outside Gary	201
Beat the Drum for Me Nicky	202
Sweet Sue, Pennsylvania (a song)	205
A Long Long Time (a song)	207
Poem: Stars under his feet	208
Out of the Rains	209
History is Beautiful	211
Afterword	213
Acknowledgments	217
Micheline's Books	
Anthologies	
Reviews of Micheline Over the Years	223
Charles Bukowski on Micheline	
Concerning the "Skinny Dynamite" Obscenity Case	
The Land of the Savage	241

Biographical Note

JACK MICHELINE, née Harold Silver, aka Harvey Martin Silver, was born on November 6, 1929 in the East Bronx of New York City, of Russian-Romanian Jewish ancestry. He attended various schools in New York, including P.S. 47, P.S. 102, James Monroe H.S., and Theodore Roosevelt H.S. During 1947-48, Micheline served in the U.S. Army Medical Corps., and for part of that period was stationed at Fort Sam Houston, Texas. In 1949 he traveled to Israel and worked on a kibbutz in the Negev. During the 1950s Micheline would spend years traveling across the United States and working various blue collar jobs. In a biographical note he sent to the British journal *Cosmos*, Micheline wrote that he had pushed a handcart in a garment factory, worked as a messenger boy, dishwasher, farmer, actor, union organizer, panhandler, and street singer. It was during this period that his first published poem, "Carnival in Pardeesville," appeared in the *American Friends Service Committee Newsletter* in Wautoma, Wisconsin, where he worked building latrines for Mexican migrant workers in 1955. Later that year, Micheline acted in an off-Broadway production of Maxim Gorky's *Lower Depths*, at the Alhambra Hall Theatre on Second Avenue in New York City, directed by Arthur Reel. He played the role of the "Tartar."

In 1957, at the Half Note Cafe on Hudson Street in the West Village, Micheline won a poetry reading contest, the "Revolt in Literature Award," judged by Charles Mingus, Jean Shepard, and Nat Hentoff. The prize consisted of ten dollars worth of jazz albums from Mingus' "Debut" record label. In 1958 Hettie Cohen and LeRoi Jones published Micheline's poem "Steps" in the premiere issue of *Yugen* magazine along with work by Philip Whalen, Diane di Prima, and Allen Ginsberg. It was the first time the name

"Jack Micheline" appeared in print. Micheline selected the name "Jack" after his favorite author Jack London, and "Micheline" by adding an "e" to the end of his mother Helen's maiden name. Also in 1958, his first book of poetry, **RIVER OF RED WINE**, was published with an introduction by Jack Kerouac. The book was reviewed by Dorothy Parker in *Esquire* magazine.

Micheline often disavowed the Beat label, in an effort to distance himself from the apparent commercialization of the movement. He preferred to cast himself in the vagabond and bohemian tradition of Vachel Lindsay and Maxwell Bodenheim. Nevertheless, he was included in two early Beat anthologies, including **THE BEATS** (Greenwich, Connecticut: Gold Medal Books, 1960), edited by Seymour Krim; and **THE BEAT SCENE** (New York: Corinth Books, 1960), edited by Elias Wilentz, and would continue to be published in Beat journals throughout his life.

Micheline began painting with gouache in a self-taught manner during a trip financed by Franz Kline to Mexico City in 1961. He lived and traveled in Mexico with three close friends: Rick Librizzi, Bob Blossom, and Ray Bremser. In 1961, while in Mexico City, two of Micheline's broadsides, "O' Harlem" and "The Land of the Savage," were published under the imprint Third Rail by Cipriano Rivas Cherif, an exile of the Spanish Civil War and close friend of Federico Garcia Lorca, a Spanish poet and playwright much admired by Micheline. In fact, Rivas Cherif's experimental theater company "Caracol" had successfully produced the premiere of Garcia Lorca's *The Shoemaker's Prodigious Wife* in Madrid in 1930.

In 1962, Micheline's second book of poems, **I KISS ANGELS**, was published by Interim Books, edited by Jay Socin. In 1964, he edited **SIX AMERICAN POETS**, published by the Harvard Book Company of New York City, to which James T. Farrell contributed a preface. In June 1965,

BIOGRAPHICAL NOTE

Micheline self-published his first collection of stories, **IN THE BRONX AND OTHER STORIES**, under the imprint Sam Hooker Press in New York City. It was reviewed by Kirby Congdon in *Magazine*. On January 4-18, 1967, Micheline's play *East Bleeker: A Drama with Music* was first produced off-Broadway by Ellen Stewart in New York City at the experimental theater Cafe La Mama, on Second Avenue. It was directed by Alex Horn, with music by Gary William Friedman.

In late 1968, the publication of a Micheline story resulted in the arrest of John Bryan, publisher of *Open City* newspaper in Los Angeles, for obscenity. The story "Skinny Dynamite," had appeared in a literary supplement to *Open City*, no. 70, edited by Charles Bukowski and dated September 20-26, 1968. Allen Ginsberg, Hubert Selby, Jr., Stephen Schneck, Jerome Rothenberg, Don Petersen, and Norman Mailer were among those who wrote letters on Bryan's and Micheline's behalf defending the literary merits of the story. With the legal assistance of civil rights attorney Stanley Fleischman, the obscenity case was eventually dismissed.

In the late 1960s and early 1970s, Micheline published three noteworthy tributes to writers with whom he closely identified. In the December 20-26, 1968 issue of *Open City*, no. 83, he published "Notes to a Dirty Old Man" for Charles Bukowski. In the February 15-22, 1969 issue of *Open City*, no. 91, he published "The Poet Named Norse" for Harold Norse. And in the May 3, 1973 issue of *San Francisco Phoenix*, Micheline published "An Old Comrade Speaks Up for the Kerouac He Knew" for Jack Kerouac.

Beginning in 1969, Micheline would self-publish many books which he mimeographed and hand-bound in stapled folders, usually under the imprint Dead Sea Fleet Editions or Midnight Special Edition. The publications were primarily short-run editions of 100 books or less, and now are very rare. These titles include: **TELL YOUR MAMA**

You Want to be Free, Angel Baby, and **Monkey Meat Farm Poems**. Various small presses would publish six Micheline books in 1975 and 1976 including Kaye McDonough's Greenlight Press which published Micheline's story "Purple Submarine" in book form. It was accompanied by a record of Micheline reading a story, "Tigers in the Sky," and various poems. In November of the same year, Paul Mariah's ManRoot Press published Micheline's collected poems **North of Manhattan, Collected Poems, Ballads and Songs: 1954-1975**. Despite the interest by small vanity presses and the praise he received for his self-publication efforts, Micheline had difficulty attracting a major publisher. Even City Lights Books, renowned publisher of the Beats, would only publish "Pink, Red and Blue," a two and one-half page story by Micheline, in an anthology of 250 pages. The collection, *City Lights Anthology*, was edited by Lawrence Ferlinghetti and appeared in 1974.

In the late 1970s Micheline began having work published in West Germany, largely due to the efforts of Carl Weissner. In November 1977, for instance, Micheline's story "Whores, Streets, Saints and Dreams" was published in *Gasolin 23*, no. 5, in Frankfurt, West Germany, as "Huren, Strassen, Heilige und Traüme." In March of 1979, a collection of short stories by Micheline, **Skinny Dynamite**, was published in a German language edition, translated by Weissner and published by Maro Verlag in Augsburg, West Germany. The following year **Skinny Dynamite** first appeared in English published by A.D. Winan's Second Coming Press.

Micheline continued his self-publication efforts into the 1990s, but, starting around 1980, he began to hand-paint gouache covers and comb-bind or spiral-bind the books in an $8 \, 1/2"$ x $11"$ format.

In addition to his self-publication efforts, Micheline pursued other projects. He had two one-act plays, *Strange*

BIOGRAPHICAL NOTE

Girls and *Ebb Tide*, produced at Cafe Flore in San Francisco in 1977. He published a chapbook of Floyd Salas' poem "Pussy Pussy Everywhere, A Voyeur's Delight" in Berkeley, California, in 1980. Micheline is also known to have lectured on the creative process. He gave six lectures in a series entitled "From the Horse's Mouth, Towards Creative Action, the Inner Response," from February 5 - March 4, 1976 at the Goodman Building in San Francisco. Micheline also taught a poetry workshop at the Naropa Institute in Colorado on March 6, 1983, entitled "The Act of Creation: Self Liberation Through Creativity."

Micheline participated in the Naropa Institute's conference, "25 Years On the Road," which took place from July 23 - August 1, 1982, in Boulder, Colorado. The conference was held to commemorate the 25th anniversary of the publication of Jack Kerouac's ON THE ROAD. Other participants in the readings, lectures, writing workshops, and multimedia presentations included: Allen Ginsberg, Gregory Corso, William Burroughs, Peter Orlovsky, John Clellon Holmes, Robert Frank, Anne Waldman, Robert Creeley, Michael McClure, Lawrence Ferlinghetti, Herbert Huncke, Carl Solomon, Ted Berrigan, and Diane di Prima. Micheline received the prize for the "Most Valuable Performance" for his reading at the conference on July 29, awarded by Ken Babbs and Ken Kesey. The prize consisted of a bottle of scotch for Jack Micheline and a bottle of Manischewitz (kosher wine) for Harvey Silver.

Micheline traveled to Europe later that year, where he was one of about 30 invitees from over ten different countries to the "Stichting One World Poetry Festival" held in Amsterdam, Holland during November 12-21, 1982. He read at the international festival with other writers, including Gregory Corso, Mohammed Mrabet, Kathy Acker, Yuvgeny Yevtushenko, Ishmael Reed, and Alexander Trocchi. A 49-minute audio recording, made by Huib Schippers, of Micheline reading live at "Ins & Outs

Press" on December 4, 1982 in Amsterdam, was released in Europe under the title *Jack Micheline, Sinterklaas Eve in Amsterdam*.

Micheline was the subject of two video productions. In 1984 the Denver Union of Street Poets released a 28-minute VHS video, auto-documentary, devoted to Micheline entitled *A Poet of Sound — A Poet of the Cities*, which includes Micheline discussing the role of the artist, and reading and singing 14 poems and songs. It was directed by Freeman Crocker and produced by Stone River Productions in Thornton, Colorado. In 1990, Jesse Block produced and directed *Jack Micheline: Big Deal*, a 52-minute VHS video auto-documentary, which includes parts of various interviews and footage of Micheline reading and singing 12 poems and songs.

Micheline benefited from the resurgence of interest in the Beats that began in the early 1990s. In 1992, his poem "Poet of the Streets" was included in THE PORTABLE BEAT READER published by Viking Penguin and edited by Ann Charters. From May 17-June 10, 1994 Micheline exhibited his art in a group show entitled "The Beat Generation, Legacy and Celebration" at New York University's Washington Square East Galleries, sponsored by New York University's School of Education. The exhibition included work by Jack Kerouac, Allen Ginsberg, William Burroughs, Gregory Corso, Lawrence Ferlinghetti, Michael McClure, and Robert La Vigne, among others. On October 18, 1994 Micheline appeared with saxophonist Bob Feldman on NBC's "Late Night with Conan O'Brien," filmed in New York City, where they performed Micheline's poem "Hot Chicken Soup." On April 12, 1996, Micheline read with Diane di Prima, David Meltzer, S.A. Griffin, and Michael McClure at the Maude Fife Room, University of California, Berkeley, at a program honoring Lawrence Ferlinghetti entitled "Ferlinghetti, City Lights, and the Beats in San Francisco."

BIOGRAPHICAL NOTE

In June of 1997, Micheline's book **SIXTY-SEVEN POEMS FOR DOWNTRODDEN SAINTS** was published by FMSBW in an edition of 400 copies. The book, which was sold by Micheline himself, sold out by late September. The book was the largest published by him in over 20 years and managed to attract interest in his work despite the limited number of copies printed, and the lack of an ISBN number or other catalogue-in-publication information. It would be the last book published by Micheline in his lifetime.

Micheline's letters to Charles Bukowski are preserved at the Davidson Library, University of California, Santa Barbara. His other archives, which include his correspondence from Ken Babbs, Paddy Chayevsky, Alberto Huerta, Langston Hughes, Linda King, Seymour Krim, Kaye McDonough, Janine Pommy Vega, Kell Robertson, Carl Solomon, Tommy Trantino, and Carl Weissner, among others, are collected at The Bancroft Library, University of California, Berkeley, along with hundreds of unpublished poems, drawings, stories, and notebooks.

Writing to A.D. Winans on July 16, 1973, Charles Bukowski said of Micheline:

> "Mich[eline] is all right. he's one-third bullshit but he's got a special divinity and a special strength. he's got a little too much POET sign pasted to his forehead but often he says good things — in speech and poem — power-flame laughing things. I like his poems very much. I like the way they roll and flow. Jack loves the sun and the cunt and the horse and the streets, and he loves the strong and the common people. his poems are total feelings beating their heads upon barroom floors. I can't think of another poet who has more and who has been neglected more. Jack is the last of the holy preachers sailing down Broadway singing the song. He's right: they'll find him after he's dead. he's fought

hard, Al, sleeping on people's rugs, sponging, playing the clown for a night's sleep, a piece of stale bacon. but going back over all the people I've ever known he comes closer to the utmost divinity, the soothsayer, the gambler, the burner of the stinking buckskin than any man I've ever known. hand him the palm the next time you see him, and try to enclose a fiver or at least a buck, he'll probably need it. Jack has it; through all the bullshit and con and hollering, Jack has it. may the gods give him a good woman who understands him, and a better Age to live in than this castrated, de-emphasized, titless, toothless, anti-human, anti-word, anti-feeling 20th. century, amen."

In the late summer of 1997, Micheline took his last extended road trip reaching Bloomington, Indiana where he read at the nightclub "Second Story" on August 30, 1997, and worked on songs with a band named after one of his short stories "Lessick's Kid." His final readings were in San Francisco. On November 13, 1997 Micheline read with Janine Pommy Vega at the North Beach Public Library and on November 20, 1997 Micheline read during his last art show at the Solar Cafe, on Valencia Street, in the Mission District of San Francisco.

Jack Micheline died of a heart attack on February 27, 1998 on a subway train somewhere between his San Francisco home and Orinda where he was discovered by transit police at 11:10 a.m. He is survived by a son from his first marriage, Vincent, a daughter-in-law Sheri, and a granddaughter Nicole.

This book is dedicated to his granddaughter.

— Matt Gonzalez, *Editor*

BIOGRAPHICAL NOTE

The flyer made by Kaye McDonough to advertise the benefit held on Micheline's behalf at 80 Langton Street in San Francisco, 1975.

Mr Jack Micheline was born in the Bronx in 1929. He wandered across the planet for 27 long years. And fell in a ditch in Cicero, Ill. and he was reborn gravatating to poetic endeavors in 1954. He has worked as a messenger, a farmer a stock clerk in a sweater factory, a union organizer, he pushed a hand-truck in the garment center. Joined every lost cause till he found his own thing— with his rekindled hope and the beat generation he read his poems with Charlie Mingus, Eric Dolphy, Booker Irwin Curtis Shahi Hadi and others. He first book of poems had a introduction by Jack Kerouac in 1957. he began painting in Mexico City in 1960 and has shown his colorfull primitive painting in Paris, Spain, Mexico, New York Chicago, Los Angeles. He has been living in San Francisco. These last 7 years and has had five one man shows in smaller places including 80 Langton St. Coffee Gallery Goodman buildings, and Nancy Armstrong Studio in Sausalito to paint is to live

Jack Micheline

Autobiographical statement prepared by Micheline in the late 1970s.

Bibliography

RIVER OF RED WINE AND OTHER POEMS
(New York: Troubador Press, 1958); reprinted
(Sudbury, MA: Water Row Press, 1986)
book of 27 poems, introduction by Jack Kerouac

THE HORSE PLAYER
(New York: [n.p.], 1961)
single-sheet poem broadside

O' HARLEM
(Mexico City: Third Rail, 1961)
poem broadside

THE LAND OF THE SAVAGE
(Mexico City: Third Rail, 1961)
prose broadside

I KISS ANGELS
(New York: Interim Books, 1962)
book of 11 poems

THE WORLD IS GETTING BETTER, POEMS FOR JOE RINGO
(New York: Unoppressed Ink Co., [1963])
3 poems on single-sheet folded in quarters

SIX AMERICAN POETS, edited by Jack Micheline
(New York: Harvard Book Co., 1964)
preface by James T. Farrell
includes 1 Micheline poem

IN THE BRONX AND OTHER STORIES
(New York: Sam Hooker Press, 1965)
book of 33 stories, 2 poems, and 1 prose statement

TELL YOUR MAMA YOU WANT TO BE FREE,
AND OTHER POEMSONGS
([Los Angeles]: Dead Sea Fleet Editions, 1969)
5 poems mimeographed in stapled folder

YELLOW HORN AND OTHER POEMSONGS
([N.p.]: Dead Sea Fleet Editions, 1969)
9 poems mimeographed in stapled folder

IT IS NOT HERE ON EARTH WHAT I AM SEEKING
(New York: Doctor Generosity Press, 1971)
single-sheet poem broadside

ANGEL BABY
([N.p.]: Midnight Special Edition, 1971)
story mimeographed in stapled folder

PUSSY POEMS
([N.p.]: Midnight Special Edition, 1972)
6 poems mimeographed in stapled folder

LOW CLASS
(New York: Midnight Special Edition, 1972)
6 poems mimeographed in stapled folder

MONKEY MEAT FARM POEMS
(San Francisco: [n.p.], 1973)
4 poems and 1 story mimeographed in stapled folder

KUBOYA
([N.p.]: Don Donahue, 1973)
poem published as booklet

ALL AMERICAN POETS ARE IN PRISON AND OTHER POEMS
([N.p.]: Midnight Special Edition, [1973])
6 poems mimeographed in stapled folder, ill. by Dave Geiser

BIBLIOGRAPHY

HOT CHICKEN SOUP
(San Francisco: [n.p.], 1975)
single-sheet poem broadside

POEMS OF DR INNISFREE
(San Francisco: Beatitude Press, 1975)
book of 13 poems and 1 story

STREET OF LOST FOOLS
(Mastic, NY: Street Press, 1975)
book of 15 poems and 7 stories

YELLOW HORN
(San Francisco: Golden Mountain Press, 1975)
book of 29 poems

LAST HOUSE IN AMERICA
(San Francisco: Second Coming Press, 1976)
book of 16 poems

NORTH OF MANHATTAN, COLLECTED POEMS, BALLADS, AND SONGS: 1954-1975
(South San Francisco: ManRoot, 1976)
book of 146 poems

PURPLE SUBMARINE
(San Francisco: Greenlight Press, 1976)
story presented in book form w/ accompanying record

CHICAGO ROOMING HOUSE
(San Francisco: [n.p.], 1978)
single-sheet poem broadside, ill. by Ed Head

SKINNY DYNAMITE
(Augsburg, West Germany: Maro Verlag, 1979)
book of 14 stories and 1 poem, in German

Skinny Dynamite
(San Francisco: Second Coming Press, 1980)
book of 16 stories, 2 poems, and 2 prose statements

Dreamers, Hustlers, Touts, Sharpies, Greed & the Big Kill
(San Francisco: Midnight Special Editions, 1981)
reprinted as **Blue Nose Was 50-1: A Race Track Story**
story published in booklet form

Poem to the Pricrocadactile
(Olympia, WA: Rosewood Press, 1982)
poem broadside

Primer to Self-Liberation
(Kansas City, MO: Howling Dog Press, 1985)
3 lithographed broadsides, designed by Michael Frederick Annis
i. Tonight I Push My Wagon Into the Night Sky
ii. It Is Not Here On Earth What I Am Seeking
iii. Final Poem In Barcelona

Acappella Rabbi, A Jack Micheline Sampler
(Pueblo, CO: Quick Books, 1986)
book of 9 poems on folded photocopied pages w/ stapled binding

For Those Who Don't Know Any Better
Be Aware of Jackals
(San Francisco: Second Coming Press, 1987)
single-sheet poem broadside

Imaginary Conversation with Jack Kerouac
(Oakland: Zeitgeist Press, 1989)
7 poems in booklet form

Outlaw of the Lowest Planet
(Oakland: Zeitgeist Press, 1993)
16 poems and 1 story in booklet form

BIBLIOGRAPHY

A Man Obsessed Who Does Not Sleep Who Wanders About at Night Mumbling to Himself Counting Empty Beer Cans
(San Francisco: Road Kill Press, 1994)
1 story in booklet form

Eternity & Dancing on the Other Side of the Street
(Stow, OH: Implosion Press, 1996)
2 poems in booklet form

After the Races
(San Francisco: X-Ray, 1996)
story broadside

Bad, Mad and Dying: Three Fictions from Alan Catlin, Errol Miller, and Jack Micheline
(San Francisco: Synaesthesia Press, 1997)
includes 1 Micheline story in booklet form

Souls
(San Francisco: Express Press, 1997)
poem in booklet form

A Dagger at Your Heart
(San Francisco: Midnight Special Editions, 1997)
12 poems in booklet form

Sixty-seven Poems for Downtrodden Saints
(San Francisco: FMSBW, 1997)
book of 73 poems and 1 prose statement
Second edition revised, 1999
book of 89 poems and 3 prose statements

SIXTY-SEVEN POEMS FOR DOWNTRODDEN SAINTS

Beginning in the late 1970s, Micheline published numerous books of poetry and stories in limited editions. They were comb-bound or spiral-bound photocopies with hand-painted gouache covers. Even copies that are numbered limited editions often vary in contents from other copies in the same series. They are too numerous to list here.

Micheline also published many single-sheet broadsides of individual poems or stories, which were often undated or dated the year of composition. They include:

A Dream About Man & Mountains

Bright Eyes

Poem: Genius Is a Ragged Lion

Hail to My Friends Who Paint in This City

I Applied for Mental Assistance

Imaginary Conversation with Jack Kerouac

Kid Dynamite

My American Land Is Not Brave

Skinny Dynamite

Tale: It Was New Year's Eve

Tigers in the Sky

Yellow Horn

Zero Is Nothing

BIBLIOGRAPHY

*Jack Micheline in New York City with his wife
Mimi Redding's dog Socrates, 1964.*

sixty-seven poems
for downtrodden
saints

Untitled, c. 1976-80. Ink on paper, 8 1/4" × 5 3/4".

POEM

crooked streets
curve into the night sky
San Francisco 1 AM
Drag Queens whistle
we're ready
as the jets rumble on
and the voices
pour out of the bars and cafes
cash registers
and wheels
all over a nation
action is life
bright colors of clothing
always that voice and moans
at the Flea Bag Hotel off Market
Thirty years kicking death in the Ass
The fool is never ready for recognition
He is

      October 22, 1986

LONG CORRIDOR

      my mind is full of words
     my eyes like pictures
   my heart like a song
my feet like rivers
   my only ear opens like a flower
       lakes of death pour out of my childhood
         there
            is
               no
                   end
                      to
                         my
                             corridor
                                    of
                                         dreams.

From the unpublished manuscript:
Notes of the Lost Cities (1955-1962)

Jack Micheline, early 1970s.

BEAUTY IS EVERYWHERE BAUDELAIRE

Beauty is everywhere Baudelaire

Even a worm is beautiful

The thread of a beggar's dress

The red eye of a drunkard

On a rainy night

Chasing the red haired girl

Baudelaire across the sky

Your raggy pants

Laughing in the rain

Beauty is everywhere Baudelaire

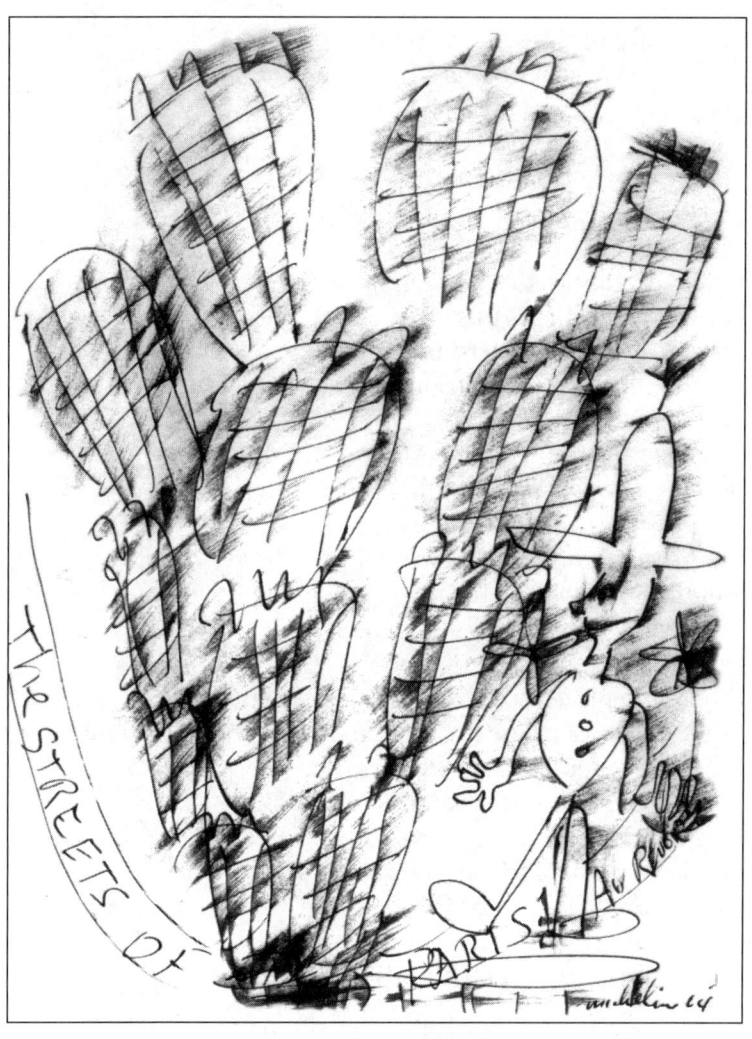

"The Streets of Paris, Au Revoir," 1964. Ink on paper, 12" x 9".

HIDING PLACES

There are hiding places in my room
where beautiful poems are hidden
Poems hidden away in boxes
on sheets of brown paper
Poems of spirit and magic
workers hands hidden in boxes
beautiful thighs
there are blue skies hidden in my room
dolphins and seagulls
the heaving of breasts and oceans
there are skies in my room
there are flies in my room
there are streets in my room
there are a thousand nights hidden in boxes
there are drunks in my poems
there are a million stars on the roof of my room
all hidden away in boxes
there are steps down side streets
there is a crazed eye of a poet in my room
there are old Arabs exploring the desert near Escalon
there are sparrows and bluebirds and wildcats in my room
there are elephants and tigers
there are skinny Italian girls in my room
there are letters from Peru and England
and Germany and Russia in my room
There are the steps of Odessa in my room
the Volga river in my room
there are dreams in the night of my room
there are flowers
there is the dance of affirmation in my room
the steps of young poets carrying knapsacks full of poems
there are the Pictures of an Exhibition in my room

Moussorgsky and Shostakovich
and Charlie Mingus in my room
Composers and painters all singing in my room
all hidden away in boxes
one night when the moon is full
they will come out and do a dance

      November 19, 1976
      San Francisco, CA

Untitled, 1996. Gouache on paper, 11" × 8 1/2".

IT IS DUSK

It is dusk and the wind is flowing through the trees
one black bird flies in the sky
blue clouds over San Francisco
a freight train is heading north
towards the Oregon mountains
a bird is singing on telephone wires
purple flower of hope
I am hope
I am the cloud and the pair of trousers
I am on the mountain above the bridges
I am the lone flag flying
that is the heart of America forgotten
I am Walt Whitman now hiring a photographer
I sharpen my pencil with my teeth
O red flower of the universe
O magic flower
get me high

      1975
      San Francisco, CA

DOWN BY THE WILD

down by the wild they are calling me
their voices enter my window
their faces, the tears of the real
I hear their voices, their lonely voices
their faces hovering in the dark
they stand under trees
across from the wild
under the lit windows
the restless children of the earth
shed tears in the face of the real
their voices enter my windows
they stand in the shadow
down by the wild they are calling me

1956

From the unpublished manuscript:
Notes of the Lost Cities (1955-1962)

*Cover of Micheline's book **North of Manhattan, Collected Poems, Ballads and Songs: 1954-1975**, published by Paul Mariah's ManRoot Press in South San Francisco, in 1976, in an edition of 1,200 copies (200 of which were signed and numbered hardcovers without dust jackets). The cover photograph is by Ira Nowinski.*

MY HEAD

My head bloody American death crying in my belly
My head full of chaos
My head bent by the years
My child's head swimming in the sea
My God's head
My life is my head
My head over the cities
My head throbbing with pain
My head filled with great souls
My head with poems unwritten
My head alive
My head full of flowers
My head in the rain
My head exploding
My head running wild in the streets
My head of love
My head of madness
My head of exultation
My head of dead fishes
My head above the Bronx
My head in many directions
My head of New America
My head full of fire
My head clear in the wind
My head of joy
My head will sing
My head always singing
My head full of gypsies
My head in black gutters
My head around the clock
My head in a tree of birds
My head of devils
My devil's head

My head of anger
 My head riding in the sea
  My head full of doubt
   My head holy
     All is my head bobbing in the wind
      All is my body attached to my head
       All is God and my head
        All in the desert
         All is all
          My head is all
           My head in the sky above cities
             On earth there is and not in heaven
            My head in the wind
             My head of grass
              My head of flowers
               That is all my head…

            Winter 1967
            New York City

POEM

I
am
a
poet
who speaks
with his eyes
and has a sad face
To
be
a
poet
is
to
be
mad
On
a
train
to
Coney Island
we
passed
a
cemetery
filled
with
dead
jews

From the unpublished manuscript:
Notes of the Lost Cities (1955-1962)

Jack Micheline, 1996.

*Micheline on University Place in front of the Cedar Tavern,
New York City, July 25, 1959.*

POET OF THE STREETS

I walk east of Bleecker
the sky is blue
on this Sunday evening

there is something deeper than the earth
there is something deeper than the stone cities
there is something deeper than our existence
than all the robes of power

power and the night bleeding gutters with crutches
power and the night and the neon vibrating
the night and thirty moons and sharpies
the night and the railroad yards gleaming
the night and the sky
the night and billboards and darkness

across a nation skeletons and machinery
jaundice, joints and lips of connivers
burnt Christmas trees
jazz horns and drummers

above concrete
above whimpering voices
above calculators
riders with tokens in their hands
riders to the sea

a nation of cowards
cowards wrapped in academic cloth

over all in darkness
over all who live in deserts
over all shells covering
over all that are wasted

burying all in nothingness
burying all that is soul
burying all with layers of armour
burying herds with still voices
burying all in the nowhere of silence

herring and fish in cans
turkey and chicken in cans
humans in cells of unknowing
there is more to life than the lights of savage civilizations
there is more to life than all the words spoken
there is more to life than the eye can see

I see the sun of angels
hemp and sugar and wheat
blood and sinew within the flesh
ticker tapes, grey hair, jowls on faces
dollars and gods and people sold and traded

people dying for nothing
people selling their minds and bodies
people without courage
people with no teeth in drug stores

death loaded with goods
givers of death and more death
cranes and deep hookers
cutting shears for the young
newspapers stunting the mind
dollars the spoiler of ships of bananas

I see your faces as I stroll through the cities
the wind touching the faces of whores
the vision of poets encompassing all
songs of children outside the brick houses

there is nothing deeper than life and the livers of life
mankind raped in the bank vaults of steel
dead soldiers, battlefields surrounded by iron and ironies

a million lost sunsets
a poet unconquered with the legacy of Whitman and Lorca
a poet unconquered by stone, by glass, by greed, by madness

the lights blaze on in the night
lights and the cold wind
visions above all death
cows milked dry, golden crosses
the sky blazing with miracles

a poet walks in the cold wind
his head raised humble and unafraid
death around him filled with waste and banners
death all around him
walking alone with birds above the canoe shaped moons
sounds are heard and the sky glows in darkness
I am not afraid.

>January 31, 1960
>East Bleecker
>New York City
>
>This poem turned the tide of my death,
>written on First Avenue off the Bowery
>in an alley of great souls.

UNDER THE STANDS

He gave out a yell and a cry
The horses had finished running
The crowd had gone home
The wind began to blow
The stands lie deserted
In the mass of twirling air
Losing tickets on the ground
The rising hoofs above his head
Hope, Death, Money, Power, Despair
The dreams of the lost and the damned
Number one for a lost home
Number two for a woman
Number three for a God without a face
Number four for a phony priest
Number five for Virgin Nuns
Number six for a longshot and a hunch
Number seven for a machine age
Number eight for the losers
Number nine for a long winter
Number ten came in last
Number eleven fell and broke a leg
Number twelve cracked up under the stands

      March 12, 1968
      Los Angeles, CA

Micheline betting on horses at Golden Gate Fields, Albany, California, 1981.

© Photo by Chris Felver

ALL PEOPLE ARE ENSLAVED

I tell you
I tell you
All people are enslaved
I tell you
I tell you
All people are enslaved
in these modern times
the people are so nervous
the people don't believe
the people feel so insecure
All people are enslaved
All people are enslaved
I tell you
I tell you
in these modern times
the people are so nervous
the people are so ill at ease
in these modern times
people don't believe
people don't believe
All people
All people
All people are enslaved
I tell you
I tell you
All people are enslaved

>From the unpublished manuscript:
>*Notes of the Lost Cities* (1955-1962)

Poems of
Dr Innisfree

Jack Micheline

*Cover of Micheline's book, **Poems of Dr Innisfree**, published by Beatitude Press in San Francisco in 1975. Jack Kerouac referred to Micheline as "Doctor Johnson Zen Master Magee of Innisfree" in his introduction to **River of Red Wine**. Micheline's title is taken from that reference with 'Innisfree' representing "in-us-free."*

POEM TO THE FREAKS

To live as I have done is surely absurd
in cheap hotels and furnished rooms
To walk up side streets and down back alleys
talking to oneself
and screaming to the sky obscenities
That the arts is a rotten business indeed
That mediocrity and the rage of fashion rules
My poems and paintings piled on the floor
To be one with himself
A Saint
A Prince
To Persevere
Through storms and hard-ons
Through dusk and dawns
To kick death in the ass
To be passed over like a bad penny
A midget
An Ant
A roach
A freak
A Hot Piece
An Outlaw
Raise your cup and drink my friend
Drink for those who walk alone in the night
      To the crippled and the blind
      To the lost and the damned
      To the lone bird flying in the sky
Drink to wonder
Drink to me
Drink to pussy and dreams
Drink to madness and all the stars
I hear the birds singing

      May 16, 1975
      San Francisco, CA

Micheline with poet Bob Kaufman (b. 1925, New Orleans, LA — d. 1986, San Francisco, CA), author of **The Golden Sardine**, **Solitudes Crowded with Loneliness**, *and* **The Ancient Rain: 1956-1978**, *Washington Square Park, San Francisco, May 29, 1974.*

POEM TO A DEAD PIGEON

Grey and white feathered bird
You lie there dead
for all to see
in the sunlit morning

Most people pass you by
for you are a dead bird
grey and white
your feathers in the sun

The Negroes pass
The West Indians
The poor Irish going to Portobello Market

The green stocking girl
who sells her wares on the corner
bananas and dates and oranges
they are selling in the market

I bend down
on my knees
in the sunlit morning
and kiss your wing
grey and white
gleaming in the sun

No more
shall you aspire
air and cloud and sky

No more
The noises of the rabble
to wet your thirst

No more
on this earth
poor bird
shall the light
blind you to darkness

No more
poor
bird
No more

        October 20, 1964
        London, England

Micheline at the Viking Hotel, 1878 Market Street, San Francisco, where he resided for much of the 1970s.

LONG AFTER MIDNIGHT
For Charles Bukowski

He was screaming in the cemetery long after midnight, the black birds circling above his head. He was laying on a cot at a county hospital, fourteen quarts of blood entering his veins in 1949. He was sleeping on a bench in El Paso, and snuck into the public library to read Fedor Mikhailovich Dostoevski. He lay drunk on an L.A. street, kicked in the face by a crazy Mexican. He lost his keys, his wallet, and I.D. He sat in a truck on Alvarado Street with fourteen poor whites and nine rednecks racing to the fields to pick walnuts. He pissed in his pants during the fifth race at Del Mar when his horse broke a leg in the stretch. One day at Santa Anita, his arms outstretched over the electric tote board, the poor bastard, waiting for the last official flash and racing to the 10-dollar window only to get shut out because the drunk in front of him didn't know what number to play. He stood in front of the schemes at the post office for nine long years beating his meat. He stole postage stamps to flood 500 small magazines with his insane poems about reality and bullshit and Mickey Mouse of what America is really about. He let his meat rot in his icebox, letting it get green with envy. He let the gold fish swim in his bathtub. He shot twenty-seven loads of cum into his typewriter. He sang the German national anthem, Achtung! Uber Eber Alles, and was the first real submarine commander of the American underground fleet. Stationed under water with his bread crumbs, he fed the birds by his porthole. He ate Tootsie Rolls and Baby Ruth when he was broke; fucked seven drunk women; and led the Bullshit Team at L.A. High School. He is the longest shot that ever came home—Scarface himself, Slit Eye, a German, a Jap, the Pisser.

He has a clean line, a clean mind, a shy inward fellow who is way ahead of all of us. His mind is calculating, a Rabelaisian, cunning and childlike and ruthless. He is not a DIRTY OLD MAN, he has never been a DIRTY OLD MAN. He is an American postage stamp, a screamer, a mark, a submarine. He gave me a dollar and kept ten for himself. Horses up his ass! Horses up his ass forever! He is the longest shot that ever came in, a highly intelligent and dangerous animal who has written seven of the finest poems in the English language today. His soul is at the fifty-dollar window and he deserves to go to the track four days a week. He deserves all the fame, money, and pussy he can eat. His shade is down on De Longpre and on the boulevards of Paris his shades are down.
He is a freak
an ass hole
a pussy-eater
a hammer
a fly
he is the green onion of Alvarado Street
a pussy-willow in the night
he is a Chinaman
a geek
a rubber duck
he is the engine that fell out of his car
he is a Polish sausage
he is the tormentor of the weeper Harold Norse
he is the maker of obscene phone calls
he is a child, a rubber stamp
he is a cockman of his dreams
he is Santa Claus and Hitler — a Charlie Chaplin
he is the green fly in your soup
he is a mocking bird
he is a bent hawk with one eye

his small pecker is a cognac bottle
he is the Pope
he serves Himself
he is one of the finest poets writing and breathing today
he is the beer bottle
he is Quasimodo
he is stone face himself
he is the freak of L.A.
he is the hunchback of Hollywood Boulevard
he is kind to his daughter
he is kind to his daughter
he is kind to his daughter
all he is folks is a glass of water
and the longest shot that ever came home.

    c. 1971

B TRAIN

The Jackson park train
roared over the south side of Chicago
by the gospels of fire
I saw black babies in the dark
among playgrounds of children
the tree of life bloomed
sparks of wheels
flew in the sky of summer
The B train roared singing a song
Savannah
Augusta
Jacksonville
Tallahassee
city
of
refugee
children
I
saw
black
babies
in the dark

       1960
       Chicago, IL

       From the unpublished manuscript:
       Notes of the Lost Cities (1955-1962)

ON COLUMBIA HEIGHTS

Manhattan
the cradle rocks in your sleep
what violin plays beneath your bridges
a ship goes out into the harbor
the massive stone against the blue waters
a heart beats
the sun eats at my brain
to and fro the waves rock back and forth
the waters engulfing the multitudes
a child
a window
a sigh
a groan
the lips of lovers
the sea rain
the sea

    c. 1963

The flyer advertising a reading in 1978 by Micheline, Bob Kaufman, and A.D. Winans, author of **Carmel Clowns**, **The North Beach Poems**, *and* **The Charles Bukowski/Second Coming Years**, *at the Neighborhood Arts Theatre, located at the University of California Extension, San Francisco.*

For Lawrence Ferlinghetti
     The Eighth Street Bookstore
     Le Roi Jones
     The New York School
     and the Black Mountain Boys

STATEMENT ON POETRY

If

I said poetry is a game
to milk the rich
I would be called a scoundrel
a liar
and a communist
Poetry
is
the aspirations
of
the
unbelievable real
We will burn the bridges
and build our own
Poetry
is emotion
a concerto
for the ears
for the eyes of the blind
It is not the bullshit of semantics
find truth in your soul
and nourish the flowers

Fall 1961
New York City

THE DEAD ARE GONE

The dead are gone with the children on the benches
the sea weeps with the cries of nightingales
and the bleeding heart drops wine on the tongue of nations
I child poet have sought in the spires and mud of cities
the rose of love and the vine of pain and forgetting
no more shall I follow the feet of birds and giants
left limp and ragged blinded in the rain to die
the masses go off weeping to wars
I child poet bitten by the cone of lightnings
left limp and ragged I crown my tears with blood
when I die the tongues of dogs will lick my wounds
when I die the leaves will fall unrelenting

>June 1960
>Washington Square Park
>New York City
>
>From the unpublished manuscript:
>*Notes of the Lost Cities* (1955-1962)

MY CITY

My city weeps for its dead
My city cries in its pain
My city is a child that cannot wait for dawn

My city is a horn
  a magnet
  an empty glass of beer

My city is a lost child
  a window
  a siren

My city is a river
  a rooftop
  a star

My city is a lover
  a piano
  a singer
  a horn full of jazz

        From the unpublished manuscript:
        Notes of the Lost Cities (1955-1962)

Micheline performing with saxophonist Bob Feldman after the production of Micheline's one-act plays, Strange Girls *and* Ebb Tide. *Photos taken at Cafe Flore, San Francisco, 1977.*

City

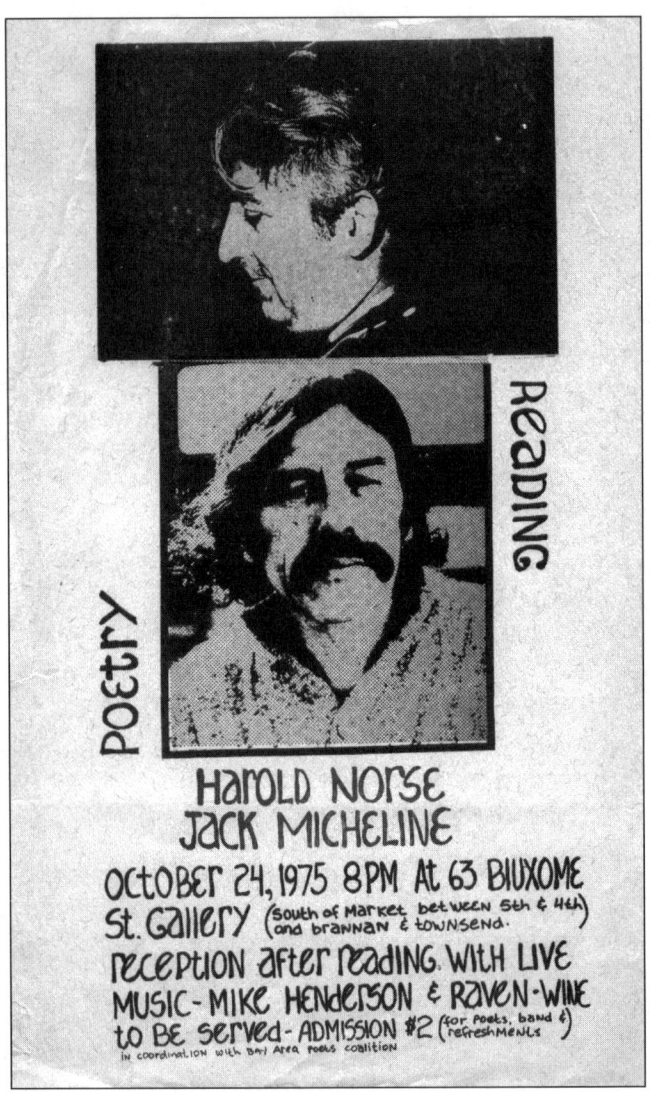

Flyer advertising a reading by Micheline and Harold Norse, author of **Hotel Nirvana**, **Carnivorous Saint**, *and* **Memoirs of a Bastard Angel**, *at 63 Biuxome Street Gallery, in San Francisco, October 24, 1975.*

TO THE ALWAYS HUNTED
For Lee Forrest

I write you a letter, rose of the saints
from a bench on Sheridan Square
from a bench in the woods where America bleeds
from its pig iron feet in the night filled with sky
what has blinded our eyes
that we go east with the wind that blows west
what fruit have we eaten
what shame do we hide
what horror, what beauty
what tears have we poured in the gutters of night
what demons within us chase us around
what angels in the night hide our faces
what lights do we hold in all darkness
the torches of fire that brighten dark cities
what terror is fear in the minds of the righteous
what judge cannot look in the mirror of saints
they shiver, God's children, O rose of the saints
the lovers that weep in the soil of eyes
which blinds us to limp and ragged of mind
the air of machines going nowhere
we are born in an age where blossoms are rare
where hunger is lonely as trees
where ghosts are not demons
where voices give joy
where voices are blinded and cry
where hearts seek the bridges of sky over water
what soul plays the strings of a junted guitar
I poet of streets that fly over mountains
send flowers to soothe your rare soul
your face and your lips filled with pain
I send you petals to cover your brow
white lilies to spread in the cells all around
in a cell where you sit and dream of your lovers

O God what a world, O rose of the saints
torn minds and red eye of the night
we will live our childhood dreams to the end
never denying what suffering means
agony, loneliness, torment and torture
lie upon lie and knife upon knife
born in infernos that tear us and bleed us
this earth like a toy that never stops spinning
this den called the earth of whoredom and madness
we are but children who play with the devils
blue Christs hung upon the cross of broad daylight
sing the blues of lament, O rose of the saints
what fruit have we eaten
what shame do we hide
we go east with the wind that blows west
we are God's children that fly over mountains
we are the children of God!

        Fall 1960
        Sheridan Square Park
        New York City

EVERYWHERE I GO

Everywhere I go is beauty
trees illuminated
street lights glowing in darkness
I want to run up to strangers and kiss them
but there is too much noise
men kill each other
I'm sick and tired of seeing sad faces
stop that bastard machine
everyone is God and Holy
a spike is ripping at my throat
I smell a fragrance of a rose
everywhere I go is beauty

    1958

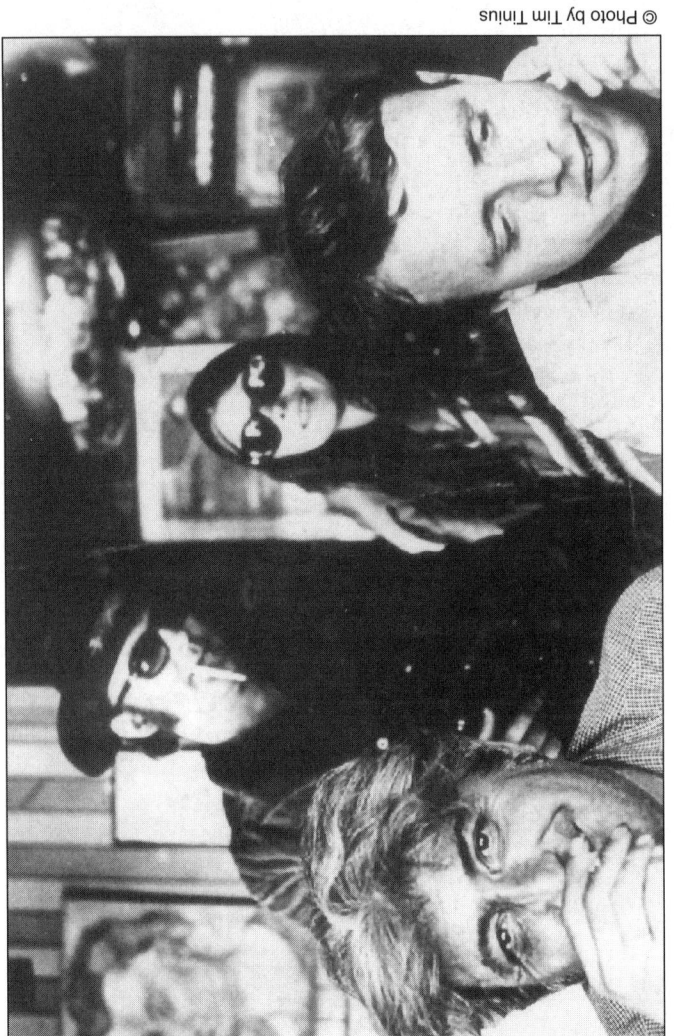

Photo by Tim Tinius ©

Micheline with poet David Plumb, author of *Drugs and All That*, *Elephant Knees*, and *The Music Stopped and Your Monkey's on Fire*, at Vesuvio's Cafe, 255 Columbus Avenue, in San Francisco. Poet and songwriter Kell Robertson, author of *Between Standing Up and Sitting Down*, *Thunderlip Jones*, and *A Horse Called Desperation*, with his wife Cindy in background.

POEM

I chose the whippoorwill

The imaginary throne of ego madness of fantasy land

I chose the herringbone

I chose the waitress at Tina's

I chose chasing pussy over a bank account

I chose poetry over standing in line at the opera

I chose art just to kick the dark devil in the ass forever

I chose pain and torture because I'm a masochist

I chose alcohol and cigarettes over 9 grain cereal

Sublime destiny over mediocrity

Like Darwin I chose the monkey over man

I chose the harmonica over the harpsichord

I chose Superwoman over Betty Grable

I chose the safety of failure over the Winner's Circle

    From a letter to Tony Dingman
    October 19, 1990

A SONG TO CELEBRATE LIFE

The wings of my skull soar over fire escapes
kites fly over cities
lovers on stoops in each others arms
tambourines roar like freight trains
death is a cancerous thing
I celebrate life
the tongue of an apple in the cheek of a brown girl
her wild skirt embroidered with flowers
her legs in the war of cities
life hangs by a thread of an unafraid eye
like a friendship that is pure as true kindness
bridges rise and unite land over water
how limp is the heart in despair
poets bury themselves
they hide from the heart
full of pity and fear and dust of the blind
wisdom is aged full of pain and beginnings
full of throbbings and fears
the joy of a sunset and sensual strolls
the wings of my skull fly over cities
I assassinate death
the one-eyed dice of a loser
the coffins of life buried with earth and nail
and the swing of lost hammers
I lift the bar of my soul
I celebrate life
I celebrate the soul
the animal night
my animal eyes
I fly over cities
John Henry had a soul and a hammer

"Ferdinand Magellan," 1980. Gouache on paper, 31" x 21¾".

TO BE A POET IS TO LIVE AND DIE

I will plant the seeds of life
where the children play
I will plant the seeds
in the fertile ground
I will plant the seeds
in the ridge rocked earth
Sunflowers shine gold
Eyes open but do not see
The flesh is covered with cloth
what you are you are
rock of the mountain
rock of the mind
rock of the silent crowds
who scream with voice
so empty I can cry
shallow beat
beat of death
beat of dying sounds
beat of this world
I laugh
I hear sounds vibrating
in my brain
I sang a song
when I was drunk
when I was high
but never dry
Song of the horn
sweet song of the ram
I hear your sound
There is always a beginning

But never an end
color of black
color of yellow
If you have not died
you were never born
If you do not feel
you are stone
O rock of the brain
Rock me to sleep
Beat of the yellow sun
Beat of the black earth
I hear your cry
O beat of the yellow sun
Shine Gold
Shine Gold

    c. 1957

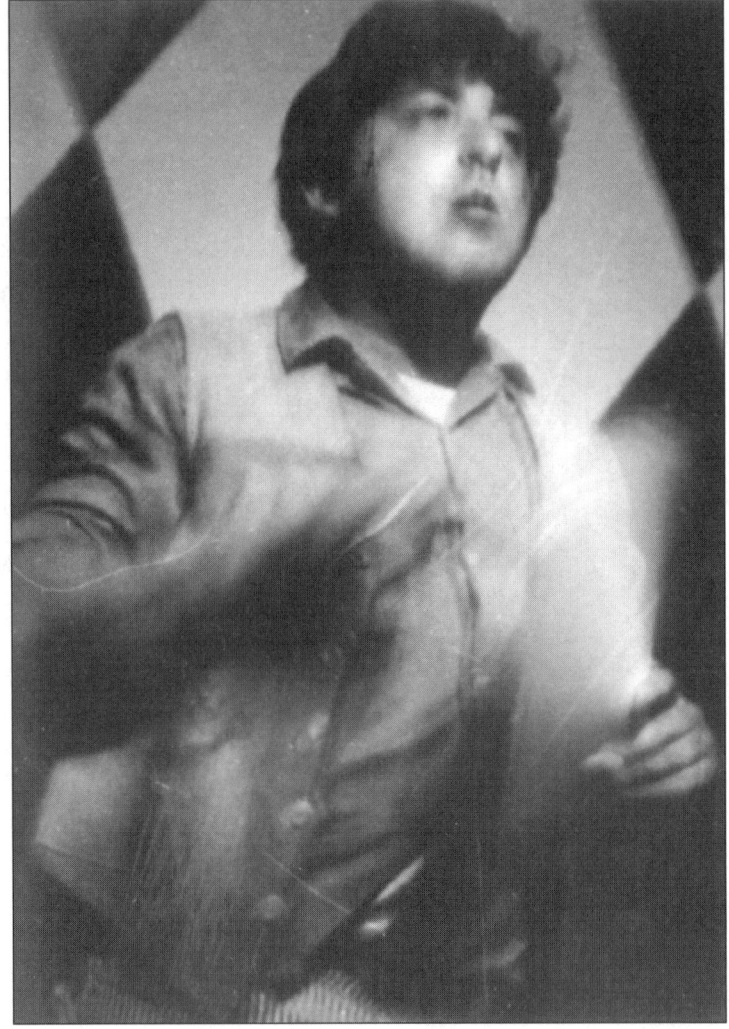

Micheline reading at the Coffee Gallery in North Beach, c. 1969.

THESE STREETS I WALK UPON

As a young boy
I remember wandering in the Miami night
the laughter of midnights from the negro shacks
the lights of darkness shone like daylight

the bars were heavy with pain and wild sounds
their faces cried for a blue Christ
walking in the streets with me
the poor were like blind men
the stars other planets
the strollers made their own music

ever since then I have been hungry for life
ever since then I have wandered
to find the secret of beauty and creation
ever since then I have refused to die

sometimes in my misery
I would pray for death to come and take me
but always a face would appear and save me
strangers nodded and held out their hands
and then I would go on again
among the beggars, outcasts of the city
where I saw real love even in death

there were no formulas, equations, recipes for life
no coverings that will save us
only the present yearnings of the world beckoned
no one being had the answer
no one being was king
a belief in some strange dream of childhood
which weaves like a crooked arrow
a directionless path through the cities

which one knows his brothers heart?
which crime have we committed in this dark world?
which love have we denied?
which fear has closed the denial of all living life?
which roads have we traveled before but we cannot go back?

sometimes I think I am not of this world
It is so unbelievable
that man can destroy without conscience
but it is so
murder in all forms around us
that greed like a dark cloud covering all fruit

yet it is light and beauty and love that will save us
why must we go on dying in the cities of pain
the staggering multitudes eat the produce of sun and rain
why must we go on dying
when our very being is light itself
These streets I walk upon speak of light!

       February 1960
       New York City

*Cover of Micheline's book **Street of Lost Fools**, edited by Ray Freed and published by Street Press in Mastic, New York in 1975, in an edition of 300 copies. Later that winter, Freed burned 30-40 copies of the book to heat his studio in Westhampton Beach, New York.*

POEM TO APOLLINAIRE

I send you a lily of Paris
O brave Apollinaire
Cities above the dull roar
The ladies who walk in solitude
The fat faces of the bourgeoisie
Who cannot nourish a rose or a chipmunk
The walkers O Apollinaire in the gray night
Where only the moon is yellow
Stars above the brightest eyes
The boulevards with the smell of spring
Her hair was dark
A well formed body with movements of a gazelle
A corner for bed sheets
A pillow
Her hair in the limelight at dusk
Brave, a poet's life like tears of lost rainbows
The ships dock at Le Havre and Marseille
Sailors drink with workers
And waitresses flirt with children
The houses of the poor at St. Germain
La petite fleur du bon
The walkers down dark streets
Your footsteps in the rain
Your shadow a poet's eye
Winter's bitch cuddled in rooms
Windowshades like sheets of rain torn from a sky
Eagles above your grave
O gray Apollinaire
The mountain peaks shine like the brightest sun in Alsace
Memories die at the graveside
With walkers down dark streets
O gray Apollinaire
Alphonse

Louis
Genevieve
The metro soars over a bridge
And the sun roars volcanoes
The wings of lost pigeons curl against your grave
Au Revoir

    February 22, 1964
    New York City

FOR GENET

in the dust
in the gutter
in the sun

in the dung
in the piss
in the prison
in the ass
you pissed in the sun
angels you saw

thieves
whores
drunks
queers
beggars
bastards
the light of this world
in the ass
in the belly
angels and Gods

       1961
       Mexico City

Untitled, c. 1976-80. Ink on paper, 8 1/4" × 5 1/2".

POEMS ARE FOR SISSIES

What's the plan

Fucking better than wine

Cock and pussy together

Against God, police, and politicians

Make it happen

The plan is action

        truth

        fire

        and the unknown

Poems are for sissies

Ass for birds

This world needs more waterfalls

        1978
        San Francisco, CA

Micheline in front of the Coffee Gallery, 1353 Grant Avenue, San Francisco, with fellow poets: Bob Kaufman; Janice Blue, author of **In Good Old No-Man's Land**; *David Moe, author of* **Plug In the Electric Dictionary** *(introduction by Micheline),* **Ishtar Robinhood Fuck Spelling**, *and* **Jazz Pajamas**; *and, unidentified woman, 1978.*

TO MY GRANDFATHER
Louie Silver Lipinsky

You sat in your room
amidst the towers of the city
and read your books of Hebrew
absorbing the sages of wisdom
and mystical chants.
White locks covered your hair with age.
When you walked the streets
children followed you.
You told them fairy tales
and their eyes glittered
dreams of wonderland.

      c. 1962

POEM

I kiss the dead face of a Russian girl
take down her phone number and race on
to the rummy hotel to collapse in precious sleep
running my ass ragged across the nation
what can we say man brother
I hear the damned singing with angels

    1969
    New York City

POEM TO FERNANDO AND THE SKY OVER PARIS
For Fernando Vega and Janine Pommy Vega

The sky is coming over Paris
The hands
The lips
The fingers move
Fernando's eyes
Peruvian painter
His eyes
God only knows
Where he has been
And what he has seen
Fernando lost
Child of the world
Is the sky over Paris
Love is not a word
It is everything
With the slow movement of the hand
The world cannot kill such a man
He can only destroy himself
But he loves
And he paints
Gone to the depths of love
Down on the ground

        October 29, 1964
        Paris, France

Fernando Vega, painter (b. 1932, Lima, Peru — d. 1965, Ibiza, Spain). Photo taken in Paris, France, 1964, shortly before his death by heroin overdose.

THE INDIGENT SOUL

he likes ice cream

he goes around with his fly unopened

he carries no handkerchief

he eyeballs the ladies

sometimes he chases them down the street

he plays horses

goes to the dirty flicks

he writes poetry

he steals his art supplies

occasionally he goes on his knees and paints

he talks to god because most

people are sad and boring

he is a fast man

he races most of his life

he toys with the world

he loves children

   1994
   San Francisco, CA

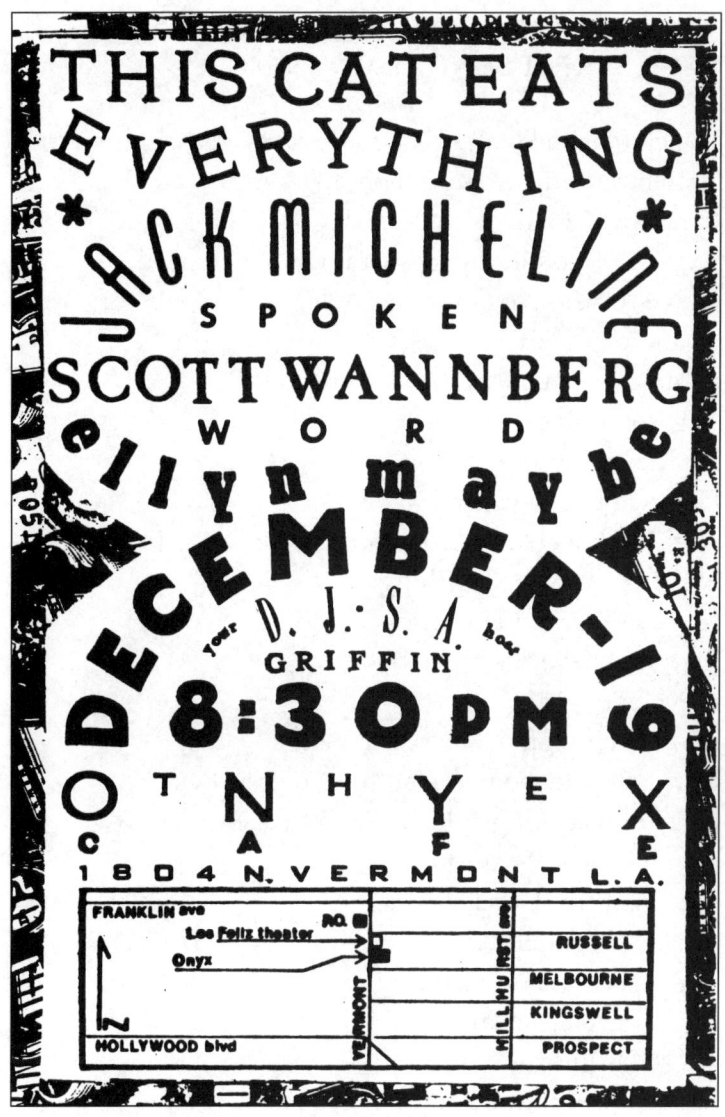

Flyer designed by Andy Takakjian advertising a spoken word event featuring Micheline, hosted by S.A. Griffin, at the Onyx Cafe in Los Angeles, c. 1992.

POEM WRITTEN ON A HOLLYWOOD BACK STREET SUNDAY MORNING

The clothesline in the backyard waves in the light rain
Nine birds sing on the telephone wires
I love and I hate
So intertwined in my foggy brain
I have traveled too much
drank too much
dreamt too much
sang too much
loved not enough
I have not been trained to kill
Nor do I kneel to my contemporaries
Nobody owes me anything
Nor can I write love letters
Man will never be big enough
brave enough
humble enough
he is a frightened nerve at the end of a stick
he is forever hungry, lost, frightened soul
love me, he says, the poor bastard
I am Federico Garcia Lorca
    Francois Villon
    Charles Baudelaire
    Vachel Lindsay
    Marquis de Sade
I am a boxer in the 9th round
A horse in the stretch
A naked man howling at the sky
A poor poet dreaming of suicide

An anarchist making bombs
My bombs are poems that cut at eye sores
I have been imprisoned by a mad dream
The flowers say hello
So does the dog and sky
Even the rain that comes down on my head blesses my heart
I have been paid off by my gift of poetry
This heat of creation
Hey world
I give you
beauty
anger
madness
a wild dance
Some poems written on scrap paper
Hey world I got light in my brain
Hey world I want to sell light
Sell light Man!
What are you crazy or something?
Who's gonna buy light?
you're no electrician
you got to write dirty stories about cunt and sex maniacs
about guys who jerk-off and carry shit in paper bags
you got to write about hang ups, losers, touts, nymphomaniacs
No!
No!
No!
I look up at the sky, the birds have gone, flown away
An ambulance races down Vine Street
My pants are ripped
I got a sore ass

I'm gonna write Carl and tell him I love him
And Bob
And Charlie
And Harold
And Sam
Tell 'em all I love them
Fuck the suicide
It's too dramatic
I'm gonna learn to write love poems
Yes!
Yes!
Yes!
Yes!
Yes!

  February 23, 1969

*Micheline with poet ruth weiss, author of **Steps**, **Gallery of Women**, and **Desert Journal**, and North Beach bartender Deno Petrucci at a party in San Francisco celebrating the publication of weiss' book **Single Out**, 1978.*

ON FRANZ KLINE

He was a clown of immense proportions, the last soul in a modern age. A pathetic genius in a modern age. A limping heart. A rag. A dishrag in a wet night. Blazing eyes of a lap dog, of a husky. Of a hunted man. Mad with light.

Black and white. Red and blue. Orange and green. The nigger of narcissus. The thief in the night. The ragged beggar. The man alive dancing up the street. People running on the other side of the street. The man was too alive. So he sang songs in a bar. Drank his heart out to death. Laughed and cried. Was a human. A big human heart beating like a piston in a drum, like a drummer and a saxophone player. A man of great magnitude, of vision. A significant human being. Wore nice sports coats with his dungarees. A man with class, class of a prince. A prince of the soul, a prince of the spirit. The prince without a kingdom but the streets of New York. The Pennsylvania-born dreamer walking the streets of the Village. Drunk, singing songs, falling on his ass in Washington Square Park.

Evicted seventeen times for non-payment of rent. To beg like a dog, like a rat, to survive. A great vision, a great artist. Won awards as a figurative painter before going abstract. He was the top banana, the man who hit the home run, the man who never compromised, a man who never sold out. A man who belonged to the people, belonged to the poor people, to the rich people, to everybody. He belonged to the whole universe. He was part of the universe. Part of a cloud that went across the sky.

He lived in his dreams.

c. 1986

Three painters: Norman Bluhm, Joan Mitchell, and Franz Kline at the Cedar Tavern, New York City. Kline (b. 1910, Wilkes-Barre, PA — d. 1962, New York, NY), encouraged Micheline to travel and financed Micheline's trip to Mexico in 1961 by slipping an envelope with $1,100 into his pocket one day when Micheline visited his studio on W. 14th Street in New York City.

MY UNIVERSITY OF LEARNING

you who are judges are unable to judge
you who limit the mind are therefore limited
you who define art limit art
you who cry freedom allow none
you who need causes have not your own
you who are moral are immoral
you who cry holy are unholy
you who are restricted need boundaries
you who are critics criticize yourselves
you who have eyes, open your eyes
you who have ears, open your ears
you who think, think for yourself
you who speak of light find more
you who have courage need more courage
you who seek darkness will find more darkness
you who seek death shall find more death
you who seek light
you who refuse to die
you who liberate the mind
you are the rose of this world
this is my university of learning

> April 18, 1961
> New York City
>
> From the unpublished manuscript:
> *Notes of the Lost Cities* (1955-1962)

GREEN

Green is the color of greed and grass and leaves of trees
Green eyes on witches and bitches
Green is the color of fields and mountains
Green is the color of Bukowski's rotting cheese
   in his icebox
Green is Ferlinghetti's hat and Bill Saroyan's chest
Green is the ring around Norman Mailer's face
Green is Janis Joplin's sky and breasts
Green is the color of Jack Kerouac's pea soup his
   mother made for him
Green are my gambler's pants
Green is the color of jade
Broccoli is green, spinach and peas are green
Snakes are green, Muldoon Elder is green, Charlie is green
Rasputin was red and green, red and green make brown
Green are the eyes of cats, emeralds, jade
Jungles are loaded with green
The Greenbay Packers are green
The Green Giant is green
The eyes of monsters are green
When my ass hurts it is green
Wall Street is green
Shamrocks are green
Saint Patrick's Day is a sea of green
The priests and nuns wave green
Green goes with red, blue and yellow and off white
The sea is green
There are green hats, blouses, stockings, pants, and
   handbags
Green is a tough color

Stay away from green
It's the snot of your nostril
Beware of green guys with red hats
Currency is printed in green
Pirates wear green
The fields of the world are green, yellow, and blue
The sea is green,
A lush is green
Abundance is green
The frog is green, the fog is green
The world is loaded with green
The cat with green eyes danced up the street
Green, I love you green

       May 8, 1980
       New York City

*Micheline with poet Wayne Miller, author of **Shadows of Remembered Ancestors** and **From Meso America**, June 1973.*

ILLUMINATION

Chicago
Rock Island
Missouri
Kansas Speedway
Cleveland Oklahoma, Texas Panhandle
America Engines Flying
Ain't waiting for some Messiah to come down
Tell me I'm a poet
Mediocrity seeks the same bullshit
Art is Dead
And All censorship is against Humanity
Let the Kids rise up and make it better
Seems there is nothing but power
Chicago
Rock Island
Sacramento
L.A.
Cleveland
Columbus
Indiana, San Francisco
Sold my blood on a Frisco line
with a guy who done 7 years
For Armed Robbery
Robbed of his birth right of Individuality
The Arts ain't for us poor whites
Ain't for the Real Cats
Sorry to say I've had it
Had it up to my Neck
Walked the Miracle Mile didn't have a fucking dime
Just want to get drunk and Sing Songs

      1968
      Manhattan, Kansas

Micheline with jazz poet Ray Bremser (b. 1934, Jersey City, NJ — d. 1998, Utica, NY), author of **Poems of Madness**, **Blowing Mouth/The Jazz Poems: 1958-1970**, *and* **Drive Suite**. *Photo taken in Woodstock, New York, c. 1984. Bremser began writing poetry while in prison for armed robbery in the late 1950s. He was first published in* Yugen *magazine.*

NIGHT CITY

Above the sounds
dark cities
lie in shadows
foghorns blast in silence
prayers of lost children
by light of mountains
darkness to light
light to darkness
I stand looking
down at the city
steeples rise in magic shapes
arcs of bridges
cover the river
steam white crosses
illuminate the eye
black tar of loneliness
billboards neon red
buildings stand and fall
but man remains
like dying timbers
in a forest
man remains

on a warehouse stairway
to the moon
three empty wine bottles stand
Nuns
Vipers
Holy Mary Face
that is not yours
but you are all
madness of cities
King majesty
drunk with awe
quiet, tired, restless city
Black tar in the night
Black tar in the night

    1957
    Rooftop on Crosby Street
    New York City

Micheline with Jessica Loos, New York City.

SAINTHOOD IS FOR THE BIRDS

There is no nobility in poverty
There is too much cruelty
Shameless greed
Man is forever cunning
And cold cash leads the pack
The devil whips our asses
The devil turns the wheel of the world
The dog licks, barks and bites
The chicken runs
Don't let things slide
Find yourself a good woman
Slick the slippy
Cover your bets with hunches
Avoid the middle class
Clowns make it
Hustlers make it
Phonys make it
Carry a knife
And a handkerchief
Eat in small restaurants
Throw your newspapers
And your television away
They are owned by vested interests
They are looking for market places
Blood to bury
Brains to control
Don't envy others
Ginsberg a public relations expert
Bukowski covers his bets
Fifty dollar bill back pocket
Santa Anita racetrack 1969
Wrote great poem
Nuns, touts, grocery clerks and me

Burroughs naked lunch
Barney Rosset slipped a shoe
James Laughlin played Garcia Villa 75¢ an hour
John Martin cries on the telephone
Ferlinghetti naked in front of banks now
All are businessmen of the arts
All are American censors
The business of America is business
Money is America
    And death
   And greed
  And darkness
Put the swastika on the dollar bill
That is what man is about America
Murder of genius and the worship of Christ
Big holes to fill
Bank accounts
There is nothing out there
No natural acts
It is all a put up job
The life of an outlaw
Leads to madness
Young death in America
On the breadlines in Siberia
Leads to mumblers
Talking to themselves
Counting small change
Only rare genius, freaks, fools
And genuine outlaws
Seize the moment
Saroyan was the last romantic
Henry Miller had pussy on the brain
Maxwell Bodenheim shot to death
Vachel Lindsay shade down Denver hotel
Steven Foster froze to death on the bowery

Beauford Delaney in a french madhouse
Charles Mills talking to the lions in heaven
John Clellon Holmes a class act observing the world
Gregory Corso a gargoyle in the ruins
Ray Bremser great wordslinger disappeared
Jack Micheline screaming in the Tenderloin
Chasing his dreams and fantasies
Learn to laugh poet
Trade your poem
In for genuine love
Avoid middle class values
The big cities are full
Of con men, thieves and murderers
Small town gossips
Most people are boring
Most poets and painters
Are not real people
Have no originality
Have no sense of wonder
Most people kiss ass
Most people are not mad enough
Kenneth Patchen was a man-child
Don't be afraid to kick ass
Don't be afraid to love
Only the landlord knocks
No beautiful young blondes
Sainthood is for the birds

October 31, 1990

IN THE DEPTHS

Within sight of ragged armies
I walked the streets of my cities
Drunk ageless with the sky
Horseless riders
Sparrows
Insects of lemon rose
Swallowers of wine knee bent in prayer
This disbelief over a clothesline
Dragons I piss on
My devil's muse
Chariots
Bulls
Horses
and Eagles
These things
That make up my life
My poet's muse

POEM

The soul weeps

The soul cries

This world closed

In a world of coffins

A poet weeps into the earth

The earth covered with leaves

Tell God I'm a gypsy

*Micheline posing for "author's photo" with friends for his book **Purple Submarine**, 1976.*

WARREN FINNERTY RIDING A BICYCLE ON 4TH AVENUE AT MIDNIGHT DREAMING OF LOVE AND WINE AND FRANZ KLINE

1. I don't know
    But he rode
    Down the darkness
    Some mad happy Irishman
    Down 4th Avenue
    No teeth
    Dreams, a part in a movie
    Come on children
    Puerto Ricans
    Mad Irishmen
    Brooklyn
    Dennis Hopper
    Hollywood
    Nobody knows Warren
    A dream
    A ghost
    A Russian hard-on
    A woman who was a flower in India on Thompson Street
    Warren riding a bicycle down 4th Avenue at midnight
    Dreaming of love and Franz Kline
    He laughed his sorrow away in drink and horses
    In Kansas City, on the East Side
    At the ranch, in Barney's Beanery in Hollywood
    Softball games, midnight movies, concubines
    Brooklyn Heights, New York parties underground
    The moon was full that night
    Chicks, cunt, women
    A pair of legs, lipstick
    Cup runneth over sapphires, sirens, railroad trains

2. Tom Halley
   Harold Anton
   Joe Gould
   Making the round to the next bar
   A merry go round
   Scorpio's, Hot Mamas
   Montana, Moses
   Assyrians, Latvians
   Poles, Polamania
   It doesn't matter to be born a freak in this world
   We're all freaks freaking freaks
   Hot hands on a skinny bike
   The moon shines with tears
   A dream of a script
   A part on a stage
   A movie
   A performance, a performance
   A dance in a dungeon
   A mask
   A montage
   A make believe Halloween
   A miraculous mirage
   Richard Widmark walks down 8th Avenue
   Christmas 1963
      or 1962
       or 1961
        or 1919
   I want to get drunk
   To say Yeah! Yeah!
   I'm on parole
   A frame up
   A hung jury
   A job on 2nd Avenue
   Tomashefsky
   Paul Muni

3. Mark Twain
   Chekhov on tobacco
   Bob Blossom
   Ellen Stewart
      Bob Bolles
        Feathers and dynamite
          The cash registers
           Chayefsky
             Actors as bartenders in drag
              It doesn't matter
               The slime of New York in cemeteries
                Miles of tombstones on Long Island
                 Warren is beautiful
                  On a bicycle at midnight
                   Riding down 4th Avenue
                    With white sneakers
                     Laughing at the stars

               1963
               New York City

STONE OF THE HEART

Stone of the heart
Fires blazing in the sky
Street lights in the city after dark
Railroad trains crossing the prairie tonight
Fire engines racing down the avenues
And gutters of the soul
Concrete city of the heart
Billboards blazing with radios
Lampposts like ghosts in the night
See the city of stone
See the prisons
The towers
The hospitals
And such hells
People jumping like maniacs
Yellow cabs and wild cats screaming in the night
Trashcans with debris
See the carnival of the city street
Pants
Shirts
Books and underwear
Street calls and hunted men
Screaming

        1996
        San Francisco, CA

Micheline with A.D. Winans at a party at Books Plus for **California Bicentennial Poets Anthology** *edited by Winans and published by Second Coming Press in 1976, which included Micheline's poem "On My Way to Boston Need Five Bucks." Winan's Second Coming Press published two books by Micheline,* **Last House in America** *in 1976 and* **Skinny Dynamite** *in 1980.*

BLUES POEM

I got no smile cause I'm down
I carry a horn to blow in all these streets
A solo riff out of my head
How could you ever know I feel
So high on life and feet and ass and legs and thighs
That I can rise and dance with all the stars
And I can eat the moon and laugh and I can cry
The dark caves of cities hungry streets
The tired faces dark and dreary bent
and all the death it dies
I let it die
I lift my horn and blow some sounds
some soul for kids to come
Some unborn sun
in darker streets than mine
Magicians carry wings so they can fly
Let's blow a horn and love
Let's get on it and ride
and laugh and dance and jive
Let's shake the dead and let the downers die
The magic of the singers warms the earth
A song
A poem
Some paradise of mind
I got to smile now
I'm feeling good
The city street
The palace of my mind

>September 4, 1969
>San Francisco, CA

Micheline performing with jazz musician and composer Charles Mingus (b. 1922, Nogales, AZ — d. 1979, Cuernavaca, Mexico) at the Great American Music Hall, San Francisco, April 1977. Mingus was one of three judges who awarded Micheline the "Revolt in Literature Award" at the Half Note Cafe in New York City in 1957.

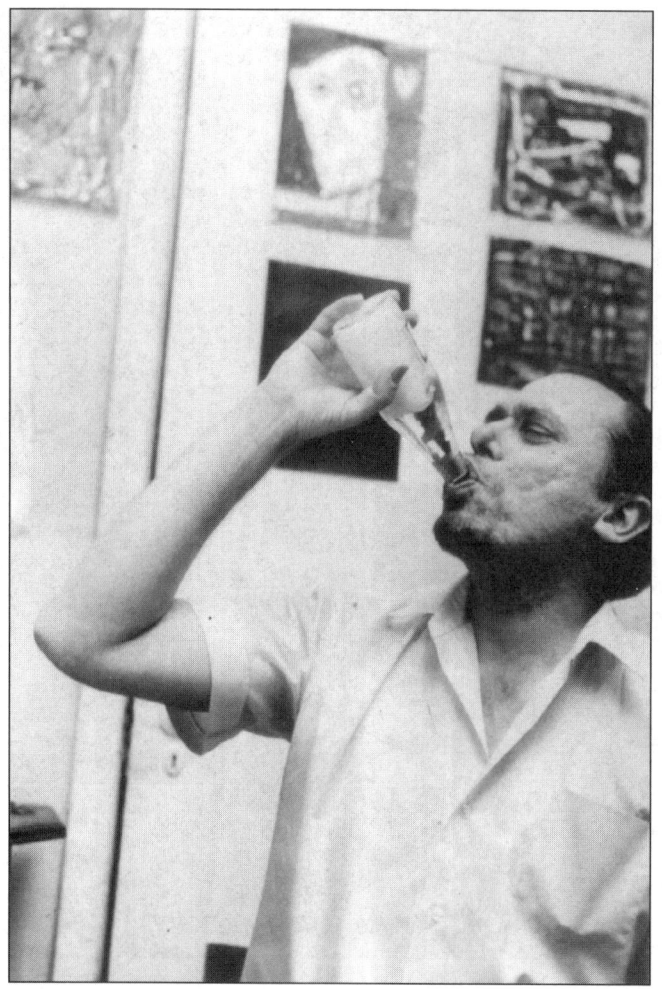

*Charles Bukowski (b. 1920, Andernach, Germany — d. 1994, San Pedro, CA) author of numerous books including: **Flower, Fist and Bestial Wail**, **Notes of a Dirty Old Man**, and **Post Office**. Bukowski was editor of the literary supplement to* Open City *newspaper in Los Angeles that first published Micheline's short story "Skinny Dynamite" in 1968. The publication of the story led to publisher John Bryan's arrest by police for obscenity. This photo was taken at Bukowski's DeLongpre Street apartment in East Hollywood, c. 1969.*

POEM TO BUK AND THE BRAVE

Part I *(Roll Over Dreams)*

He drinks to forget
Where genius lies
Some say it with a gun
Some say it with words
No gods or giants
No glory
This doing
The deed
Make words jump off a page
Make words dance off a page
The force within called creation
The eye
O wounds like a dark bull
O poet
O warrior
No nation stands when a poet is ignored
Every day a new poem
Written with his cock
The people want paper
These steel images seeking flesh
O fired brain
O truth seekers
Let the darkness roll
Roll over dreams
Lost images
The dreaming eyes beyond death
The damned sings
On the empty spaces on the plain
Empty the streets of L.A.
San Francisco
Denver

Oklahoma
New Mexico
Mexico
Conktown
Coffee and rock and roll
Visions gone forever
Twenty five years before pissing in a cell block
Pissing as the girls walk by
Drinking limp leg over a fat mistress
Drinking beer and cum forever
Let the darkness roll
The damned still singing
On a freight train
Jails
Loony bins of a nation
In furnished rooms and Nedicks
In the bored truck drivers
In the eyes of girls legs
Walking in the streets of forty states
And nations
And dreams
For five
For ten
For fifteen
Take your pick
A poet of our time
Crown tears on his skull
Crown the prince
His mind rises over the multitudes

Part II *(Crown Him You Bastards)*

Crown the poet
Bless him over tired words
And trains

And bodies of lost sighs
And lost hope and dreams
Crown him you bastards
He brings life to you
And you turn your head
Play your game
Pull your cock and die
Drink your beer
Say the same words each day
Men sucking fear
Men sucking dark death
The dark city windows and eyes
Kicking it all in the ass
Burn the typewriters
Nothing is safe or sacred
Crown him you bastards
People will kill him
The poet belongs to the gods
Streets that nurtured him weaving
The last shot
The last glass of wine
The last word
Without a pencil
He writes with his cock
Without a cock
He writes with his eye
Without hope
He writes with a dream
Without a woman
He beats his meat
Without money
He sucks the air
Without faces
Without streets
Without dreams

He is dead
He gives a shriek
A loud yell
A wailing moan
He laughs at it all
Waiting for a cool night
To strike at the pack
A poet awaits his fire
A poet waits
Crown him you bastards

Part III *(At The Races)*

At the races
The horses are on the track
It is now post time
Blue Nose three pounds over
Running Ridge kicked a shoe
Moon Glow
Hot Roll
Sentinel God
Pigeon
Flower Girl is ready
Singing Sargent out of Purple Pilot
Beau Geste pissing at the gate
The skies are clear at Hialeah and Santa Anita
Tropical
Pimlico
Bowie
Aqueduct
Hawthorne
Garden State
They're off
Pigeon goes for the lead

Hot Roll is second
Singing Sargent third
Blue Nose is fourth
Little Jimmy is screaming
Irish Red wears dirty socks
The rich blonde blew her roll and fucked the jockey
Kids piggy banks
Abortion money
Money of death and dominion
Horses hoofs
Numbers
Dreams
Rapes
Blue Nose leads the pack at the three quarter poll
Hot Roll goes to the outside
Beau Geste still pissing at the gate
People are crying and laughing
Nut House broke a leg
The dreamers played Moon Glow
He went lame approaching the first furlong
Sentinel God is on the move
And down the stretch
Forty seven thousand screaming
Its Blue Nose and Hot Roll
Blue Nose the winner going away
Singing Sargent fades to last
Beau Geste still pissing
Tickets on the ground
Mr Birnbaum lost his business
Up and down
Death and dumbwaiters
Numerals 1,2,3,4,5,6,7,8,9,10,11,12
Cover the field
Madness and dreams
Men

Machines and money
Beau Geste still pissing at the gate
Hot Roll, Hot Roll, Hot Roll, Hot Roll, Hot Roll

Part IV *(Blessed Be The Damned And The Losers)*

Brother to the damned
A poet walks
Opens his eyes
Takes a look around
God damn his eyes
He can't believe it
His eyes
Like one arm
The heart pumps blood
The eye and the brain united with the heart
Sensuous
The pencil
The paper
The poem
A million dead by machines
A million dead on the trains
A million dead in the newspapers
A million dead before twelve
A million dead of closed doors
And rheumatism and apoplexy
No saviours
No banners
Nor pacifists
Alleviate the pain of one solitary man
No last night speeches
Luke warm for morning coffee
Who will break the chains
Cut freedom with a knife

And declare one solitary word of hope
One touch of the thigh
Tell you each one is a prince
Each one to be brave
Each one to be a poet
Throw your wigs away
The clowns have taken over
This game called existence
And life a magazine
Life is to live
To live and not to die
One must assert
What one is
Destiny is
What we are
What we will be
Take that giant step
Life has always been hard
Like the cold night
Let us destroy the death within us
There are no winners
Fame
The image outside is a lie
Walk your path
The poet hurls his image at the world
At the practical railroad already merged
At the pedestal broken forever
At the plan ridden out
At the put up job
Like the chess board
IBM-BOAC
Hallelujah
Pussy on a cold night
Lost your wig man
The streets are burning
The radio blasts

How's my image man
Does it look good
Did the photographer show up
Lost gods
Fortify
Pacify
And deny
The preacher finked out
Already the judge dropped dead in his robes

    March 15, 1968
    New York City

LET'S SING A SONG

The night came quickly and the bells of churches rang.

The crowds poured out of the subway entrances
                                    to their homes.

A million hearts drawn like a magnet
                                    to the roar of time.

    Which one is his master?

        Which one smiled amidst the crucifixion?

            Which one bared the pain of pent up prisons?

I saw their faces walking down the street.

I enjoyed looking at
  swivelhipped young women
    with paint on their faces
      sorrowful eyes
        blank stares
          of emptiness
        their insides
      waiting to jump
    and their voices
  to sing a song.

It was a cold sight

  in a big city

      where love is the roar
        and death is the beat
          the beat.

And I yelled like a

    madman

        at the top of my voice

            Everybody sing

            Everybody sing

          I started to sing a song

        about pretty flowers

      then the men with white coats

    came with their jackets

and I told them to sing also

    and they took me away.

        Let's sing a song

          Let's sing a song

            and they took me away

           away

              away

                from the roar

                  and the beat

                  the beat

                    the beat.

                        1956
                        New York City

Micheline receiving award for best performance at Kerouac conference from Ken Babbs ("Merry Prankster" and coauthor with Kesey of **Last Go Round**) and Ken Kesey (author of **One Flew Over the Cuckoo's Nest** and **Sometimes a Great Notion**), Boulder, Colorado, 1982.

© Photo by Gerald Nicosia

Eddie Balchowsky (b. 1916, Frankfort, IL — d. 1989, Chicago, IL) with Mary Berger (b. 1938, Syracuse, NY — d. 1983, Berkeley, CA) in Forestville, California, 1983. Balchowsky lost the use of his right hand in 1938 on the Ebro River in Spain while fighting with the Abraham Lincoln Battalion in defense of the Spanish Republic. The injury later necessitated a partial amputation of his arm. Nevertheless, he was an accomplished painter and classical pianist.

ONE ARM

For Ed Balchowsky

He made love with one arm
He sang with one arm
He laughed with one arm
He cried with one arm
He walked the streets of Chicago
All with the one arm
Was beaten up with one arm
Went to jail with one arm
Took a shit with one arm
Played Bach & Beethoven
Sang on the rooftops
To early dawn
Old Spanish War Songs
All these things
With one arm
He made love
With one arm

One arm
One arm
One arm
One arm
One arm
One arm
One arm

Ed Balchowsky
My Friend

From a poem painting, 1974

POEM TO THE SEVENTEENTH OF NOVEMBER 1962

The eyes of children follow me as I walk through the streets
A clothesline waves in this November afternoon
The sea gulls dipping their wings in the harbor
Traffic roars across Houston Street
I just ate a potato pancake
it cost me twenty cents
O water towers
O beautiful sky
where are the angels
in the underground of cities shivering prostitutes
walk up Third Avenue
hard faces pass them by
faces of nickels and dimes and half dollars
I see aerials
drums are beating in a vacant loft
the cold air brushes against my face
history is a lie and time is a whore
The lips of dead dogs lie in the street
The twentieth century races by
and civilization is a worm that crawls sucking
Children smile at me as I walk by
their eyes like dandelions
No need to tell them what a poet is
The wagon is picking up some old rummies
One of these days I will run wild in the streets
and smell the indian corn under the pavements
The sky grows dark
The twilight is coming

O Manhattan where are the indians now
four million souls in the rattle of trains
four million
and a poet conquers a city
O city! infamous, cruel, undeserving
city of stone and lost loves
Those children's eyes
I am blind to the sky
let the light shine
It is time to stop the clocks!
Most people want to love but they can't
that is the crime
I want to be with angels!

       November 17, 1962
       New York City

THIS MY FRIEND IS HOW RARE POEMS ARE WRITTEN

The steps move the heart
The heart fuels the eye
The mirror of the brain
Listen to the rhythm of your breath
This how rare poems are written
Not with words but strange notes
That move the pen on the page
This is the eye of the storm
The earthquake
God's gift to nature
Immortality

      1996
      San Francisco, CA

Untitled, c. 1980. Ink on paper, 5" × 4".

*Cover of Micheline's book **Yellow Horn**, published by Golden Mountain Press in San Francisco, in 1975. The cover drawing is by Dave Geiser, who also provided the illustrations for Micheline's book **All American Poets Are in Prison and Other Poems**.*

RAMBLING JACK *(a biography)*

Walking in a city in a daze
I opened up my heart so I could breathe
The air of life bubbling from inside
The movement of the eye to pen and brush
A thigh
A nose
A leg
The movement of a buttock
Up the avenue of time
strolling in a morning breeze
the sun that warms the Earth
the rain and snow and wind
to be alive like comets, shooting stars
The Child's eye ablaze
The wonder of cats and bats and bells, salamanders
Flowers singing in the air
all these things
Hobos, bums, blacks, the destitute desperate desperados
Museums like graveyards without foliage
boredom, strife, fear on faces chained in buses,
    jobs and wages
football fields of cheers, frustration, anger, victory,
    pits of warfare, the Piston's pride
Teachers smug like bugs and protestants
The Artist is a force for light
I'll give you color
reds and yellows, orange, purple, green
and fifty shades of blue
treetops, chimneys, railroads, bridges, rivers, streams,
    lightning, valleys
The children live and playing in the sun
To be alive
To be is the poem

A shooting star
A submarine
This life of climbing mountains falling down and rising
A submarine submerged in depths lower than mud and
   slime reaching for stars
The dead, dying and the bored in slavery of fashion,
   food and horses
singing, crying, dancing, fighting, dying, fornicating,
   shadow boxing
I chase my ghost through city streets
Through Paris, Rome, Constantinople, New York,
   Chicago, Boston, Mexico City, Merida, Isla de Mujeres,
   New Orleans, L.A., Miami, San Francisco
I chase my dreams and out the darkness
It is fear that runs the wheel of all the world
   and keeps it turning
Madness, Power
Turning inward like pomp and ceremony
The politicians guile
The cunning, slippery eels and double dealing
   double crossing
Genius is a Freak, A dog Alone Sublime!
The shrinks have lied
Your mother lied
Your teachers lied
The Rabbi lied
Your Brother even lied
Newspapers full of lies forever
It's all a stage, A game control
No natural acts allowed called truth
I am a freak, a dog
life is not a game, a stage of clowns
O Wisdom of my heart
O pussycat
I come from clouds

From earth
From constellations
I come from heat
and dream
and dungeons
I am tired Mr. Charlie
Leave me be
Ten books
Five hundred paintings
A thousand streets
Skys, furnished rooms and cheap hotels
Rooming houses
horses dying in the stretch
and women playing Yo-Yo with my mind
I do not seek it
Fame's a bitch Goddess Cleopatra
Osmosis is the fame I seek like air and water
Infamy like floods and fire and earthquakes and legends
natural acts untarnished and pure
like bird and wing and wind
The ghost that comes from nowhere and returns
shakes the dead and dying
A dirge rising from cloud
A pair of trousers and a song
Who I am and what I've done soiled
will come in time
Enjoy the riches that you have
Ask me for my Biography
I've taught you more than most
I do not want to be acclaimed by Mediocrity
It is a fool's game called greed and war and markets
 and seduction
I do not play the game
The rules are cruel
There are no rules

No compromise!
and life is not a game
I walk the streets the richest man that ever lived
Tell Muldoon I told you so
I have the sky, the air, the bird
I have my eyes
My health
The knowledge of survival
more than most
Grey hair
The gleam of cities in my eyes
My spring like walk of feet
That I am rare
A genius freak
A bird of time
I seek no more my friend farewell
And Tell Muldoon
I told you!

    c. 1981

"Good Luck, Horses Asses," 1995. Ink and wash on paper, 7 1/2" x 6".

OLD MAID (*a song*)

I want to be an old maid
I'm an apple man
I'm a Chinaman
I'm a Frenchman
I'm a strawberry man
And I make jelly jam
I want to be an old maid

I'm a railroad man
I'm a fisherman
I'm a whalebone man
I'm a son of a gun
The girl I'm chasing
Got strawberry hair
And she wants to be an old maid

There's a thousand pebbles in the sand
There's a man with a mask
He's a rubber man
And the man with the mask
Got an adding machine
He's a rubber man
He looks real but he ain't
He's got an adding machine
But he's a machine
A rubber man
He looks real
But he ain't
Ha, Ha, Ha, Ha, Ha, Ha

Children are great
They like the sun
They know how to smile
They know how to run
They got little dolls
And slinky runs
Children are great
They like the sun
They know how to smile
And they know how to run
Hi Ya, Hi Ya, Hi Ya,
Hi Ya, Hi Ya, Hi Ya,

I want to be an old maid
I'm a strawberry man
I'm a chinaman
I'm a railroad train
I'm a son of a gun
I'm gonna bite the apple
And free all the worms
I'm gonna dance in the rain
And show you the sun
I want to be an Old Maid
Ha, Ha, Ha, Ha, Ha, Ha, Ha,
I Want To Be An Old Maid

       July 1971
       San Francisco, CA

PROLOGUE TO EAST BLEEKER

I say that night comes as a blessing
we hide our faces during the day
the pain of the light blinds the eye
we sons of darkness, we daughters of Cain
say that night comes as a blessing

our hands and our eyes awaiting the night
wild dogs, wild cats running wild in the streets
the heat of our blood always racing
we sons of darkness, we daughters of Cain
say that night comes as a blessing

out from the darkness, out into light
away from the sins and the shame of our fathers
away from the womb and the tears of our mothers
we sons of darkness, we daughters of Cain
say that night comes as a blessing

we hide our faces during the day
our bodies take shelter under the trees
wild dogs, wild cats they die on the street
we sons of darkness, we daughters of Cain
say that night comes as a blessing

out from the darkness, out into light
away from the shame and the sins of our fathers
away from the tears and the womb of our mothers
we sons of darkness, we daughters of Cain
say that night comes as a blessing

    1963
    New York City

The flyer made by Bill Barrell to advertise the off-Broadway production of Micheline's East Bleeker, A Drama with Music, *first produced by Ellen Stewart at Cafe La Mama, E.T.C. (Experimental Theater Club), New York City, on January 4, 1967. It was directed by Alex Horn with music by Gary William Friedman.*

Cover of **Six American Poets**, *edited by Micheline and published in 1964, with cover photo by Mario Jorrin and cover design by Gus Sheuer. James T. Farrell (b. 1904, Chicago, IL — d. 1979, New York, NY), author of* **Studs Lonigan, A Trilogy**, *who served as best man at Micheline's wedding to Mimi Redding in 1963, contributed a preface.*

SOMEDAY I'LL LIVE FOREVER

Someday

After the shouting

And the fashions run out

Someday

After the rain

and the burning

after the brain picking and the murder

After the mod chasing

And the heat of parties and palaces

After the cold night death

The Sun.

    c. 1968

Micheline with Kaye McDonough, author of the drama **Zelda, Frontier Life in America**, *at Caffe Trieste in North Beach, c. 1972. McDonough's Greenlight Press published Micheline's book* **Purple Submarine** *in 1976.*

A REAL POEM

A real poem bites the wind
And kisses the stars
A real poem is not in a book
It's a knockout
A long shot
A shot in the mouth
A crack of the bat
A lost midget turning into a giant
A lost soul finding its own way
After a generation of mediocrity and vipers
A real poem
Kicks the politicians in the ass
Kicks the poetry politicians in the balls
It is too hot to handle
It is more dangerous than war
It is a firefly
A rainbow for all

        May 1994
        San Francisco, CA

THESE CITIES

streets set afire

faces and subways

like all the machines

they have taken the eyes away

taken those millions for a long ride

the stone does not speak

the glass, concrete canyons of the Abyss

thousands talking to themselves

and in the bars

the devil pours the drinks

always the cash register ringing

always the night

from high above the buildings

the people look like ants

one hundred miles of stone

these cities

>1978
>New York City

STREETCALL NEW ORLEANS

way down
      shack town
            low down

Mary Lou
      Nigger baby
            washin window
                  garbage pail
                        blue
low down
      shack town
            way down
                  Nigger baby
                      blue
wagon man
      trolley car
            end of line
                  Bar room blue
horse player
      buggy ride
            way down
                  shack town
                      wagon wheel
                          blue
Black face
      Nigger baby
            buggy ride
                  Pragger St.
                      blue
New Orleans
      french bread
            nickel loaf
                  gasoline
                        benzedrine

wild night
        crazy lover
                blue

New Orleans
        fat girl
                skinny girl
                        ugly face

low down
        southern drawl
                Nigger laugh
                        blue

Black eyes
        gold teeth
                Shoe shine
New Orleans
        skin joints
                jazz room
                        Newcombe college
                                baby face
                                      blue
Shack town
        low down
                french quarter
                Decatur St.
                        hustling night
                        blue
Mail man
        Christmas time
                glass of water
                        Tulane
                              no train
                                  blue

```
Woolworth
        Canal Street
                St Charles
                        Dauphine
                                Pirates Alley
Cool night                              Rabbi Blue
        tall tree
                love ya baby
                        white school
                                black school
                                        no school
Creole                                  blue
     Mickey finn
             hot baby
                 all night
                         shack town
                                 low down
                                         way down
sittin down                             blue
         sweet face
                 lover gal
                         old lady
                                 corner kids
                                         laughin
Black eyes                              Blue
        Gold teeth
                Shoe shine

Preacher fat
         poor folk
                 drinking beer
                 preacher say
                                wait for heaven
                 poor folk
                          singing blue
```

Black eyes
        Gold teeth
                Shoe shine
Way down
        Shack town
      Low down
              Nigger Baby
                      Blue
Black eyes
        Gold teeth
              Shoe shine
                     Shoe Shine —

                          Summer 1956
                          New Orleans, LA

Untitled, c. 1977. Ink and wash on paper, 13" x 10".

SOUTH STREET PIER

The bridge had risen
above the stone and lights of Manhattan
the river weaves with wrinkles of Christs head
the red brick warehouse stands
the stevedores haul the rigs to the masts
the Kids fight in the streets
Mechanics Alley where the Rabbis sat and prayed
O chaos and pain of our youth
I am drunk with the moon
and the Mexican line swims in my mouth
There is love in my eyes
the Statue of Liberty is always in the water
Staten Island waits
the cleaning girls are scrubbing Maiden Lane
the smoke pours stacks from the Brooklyn shore
the fog horn tickles my belly
I hear the Drums beating
throw my ashes from this pier when I die.

    c. 1956

$ 2.00

JACK MICHELINE

IN
THE
BRONX
AND
OTHER
STORIES

Cover of Micheline's first collection of stories,
In the Bronx and Other Stories, *self-published under the imprint Sam Hooker Press in June 1965.*

POEM TO BOB KAUFMAN

Born in Louisiana
The wail of saxophones paraded in the sky
Black son of rain
Marched down Bourbon Street
You walked the streets of North Beach
Out of your mind
A blown mind
A golden sardine
Out of the desert concrete
Of American mythology
You went all the way
To Unknown worlds
Anything done to excess drowns us
Cuts us down like wild dogs
Nothing man has done on this earth
Will remain on this earth
Nothing but the fire of creation
The Music played down Rampart Street
The voices of the children playing
The Tambourines
The poet's eye across the Zodiac
The laughter of the children in the night
The poet walks home
Floating in the sky

        From a poem painting, 1973
        New Orleans, LA

Micheline with poet Bob Kaufman (b. 1925, New Orleans, LA — d. 1986, San Francisco, CA), author of **The Golden Sardine**, **Solitudes Crowded with Loneliness**, and **The Ancient Rain: 1956-1978**, at City Lights Bookstore, 1984.

© Photo by Michelle Maria Boleyn

Jack Kerouac (b. 1922, Lowell, MA — d. 1969, St. Petersburg, FL) author of numerous books including **On the Road**, **The Subterraneans**, **The Dharma Bums**, *and* **Mexico City Blues**. *Kerouac helped launch Micheline's career by writing the introduction to* **River of Red Wine** *in 1958. The introduction has been reprinted in a collection of Kerouac's miscellaneous writings entitled* **Good Blonde & Others** *published by Grey Fox Press. This photo was taken in Washington, D.C., 1942.*

CHASING KEROUAC'S SHADOW

The alabaster city gleams in the sunlight
I am on a bus going to Santa Rosa
Away from the stinking hotel
They tell me I am famous, like the Jerome cookies
Streets, poems, nuthouses, jails, paintings, con men and time
My twenty years of poems and paintings
stored away in houses and cellars
relentless with anger and love
I ponder at life and the world around me
The bus speeds on the highway going sixty
I am fifty-two, live alone, considered some mad freak genius
In reality I am a fucked up poet
who will never come to terms with the world
No matter how beautiful the flowers grow
No matter how children smile
No matter how blue is the bluest sky
The harsh realities of life, that life is mostly a put up job
The genius rain avoids us
The lone solitary soul that does her beautiful dance for
    all to see
I seek the genuine leaf blowing in the wind
The real person tapping a song whose melody
flows through rivers and time
The image that dances with stars
The sun that melts anger and harassment
Years spent begging and hustling
Carrying paintings on buses
Carrying mattresses through streets
Evictions, lost loves, hangovers, rheumatism, hemorrhoids
For a muse that rarely pays off
I must be mad, bewitched like a lost gambler
Down to my last bet with no carfare or candy
I am not subtle or charming

I cannot lie for money or tell stories
I'm the gray fox some schmuck
The old pro chasing the mad dream
The crazy Jew himself
Who don't know when to quit
Who can't say die unless I die
It is all a mad dream
The race track full of maniacs
Lost gamblers living on hope and dreams
Tomorrow is never better
The same buses full of beaten and tired faces
I only know when the cock rises and the crow howls
To eat, to drink, to take a leak
And chicken is good to eat when one is hungry
Money buys everybody, that is why the world is fucked up
That is why politicians have seventeen faces and
　　speechwriters
And waitresses wear lipstick
Why mediocrity rules
Why poets hang out in groups for protection
And musicians disappear faster than flies
And artists suck the rich quicker than summer watermelon
and bourgeois children
Why the communists and capitalists
Use the same deck of tricks
To hide the miraculous
The magic of life
The wonder of children and salamanders and birds
Wonder is the thunder
Wonder is the Spring rain itself
Wonder is the young girl in love
Wonder is love
The concerto
The hummingbird
The clouds moving across the night sky

It is raining again
Light against darkness
Shadows chasing the sun
The sun chasing the shadows
Man against the night
Man and woman together with the night
The day awakens
Let's sing a song
For those who chase the night
For those that dance with light
One speck of light
No matter who is light
Light the unknown
The unknown, it is all we have
Anything is possible
Like new born colors flashing across the Universe
The road
The vagabond
The dreamers
The dancers
The unsung
Fuck the Gung Ho!
Byron Hunt is doing a collage at the Goodman Building
Ed Balchowsky is doing another painting
Raising his one arm to the sky
Rosalie Sorrells is singing a song in Kansas
Sam Shepard is smiling
Rare birds are coming out with new coats of color
Rainy Cass is alive and well in New Orleans
Valentine Chuzioff is sketching some blonde in
   Jackson Square
Bodenheim hustling another poem for wine
Franz Kline singing a sad song at the Cedar
Kerouac talking to the moon again
James T. Farrell chasing a waitress at Yankee Stadium

Charlie Mingus bopping, chucking, eating a steak
Playing bass with angels
Wilbur Ware
Gil Gaulkins
Bill Bosio
Al Delauro
Bob Bolles
Charlie Stark
Sue McGraw
Linda
Charlotte
Banana Boat
Steamboat Jones
Jeremiah
Jerusalem
The light is coming out
I'll give the sun away
It belongs to everybody
It's not mine to give away
Those with the sun
Those seeking the sun
Those on the run in the Chicago night
Those in jail
Those in the towers
Those chasing a ghost in the wilderness
Those on the road
Those with dreams
Those who will never give up
Those who are learning to dance
Those perplexed
    agonized
    wacked
    wretched
    tattooed
    confused
We are all the sun

You are the sun
This world is one
Those with wonder, you are the sun
Shake the sun
We are one
The moon and the sun are brothers!

    March 15, 1982

    Written on a bus from
    San Francisco to Santa Rosa

POEM ON A DRUNKEN EVENING

The sky over Europe

The sky over Indonesia

The sky over Japan

The sky over Russia

The sky over China

The sky over Madagascar

His ass over America

His eyes over Chile

His nose over the Antarctic

His brow over Poland

His heart over Romania

His soul kicked out of every bar in town

       1986
       San Francisco, CA

PRAISE TO THE ORIGINAL MIND
WHO BREATHES FRESH AIR

It was attributed to Van Gogh that he said before he shot himself that there was "no order in life." His mind burning colors, deep reds and yellows opening modern art to the Twentieth Century. Damn the critics, the academics of organized art, or of abortion. They are on earth to ratify the status quo. Killers of experiment and imagination. Poor, suffering, unloved man, the middle has entered this art scene because there is money in it. A taste of honey fame.

O Submarine
Periscope
Hatches open
Torpedoes away
Zonk another hat
A destroyer amid ships
Blown away to the depths of the sea

It is pleasing like a young virgin sweet and honeycombed desiring, ready for the plunge. The entrance of birdcalls and stars. The weak fall by the side and die. A poet of promise shattered. A metropolis rises, falls to the decay and rot of man and time. Rooms, rats, roaches, ribald dances, alcohol, syringes, needles, pills, perversion, paranoia

Dark cities on the hill
wheat on the plain
Journals of existence
diaries of moments
recorded in an assertion of will
from that will springs all wisdom

knowledge, poetry, revolution, rebirth
in the end accepted institution ...
or madhouse, prison, jail of Baudelaire's cities of Europe.
If it does not sink, the ship comes home to port —
Hamburg
Le Havre
Marseille
Stockholm
Brest
Naples
Paris
Constantinople

I dreamt I saw a hundred Allen Ginsbergs, naked, reading **HOWL** in a window at Macy's. It is a sad affair what modern America does to its poets. Or what happens to poets in Twentieth Century America. When man's God is false he breaks and dies, the followers die but an original mind survives. Sherwood Anderson, he had a human face, wandered around the night cities of his youth — the vast Ohio and broadflat Illinois. The machine age had just come and he predicted the human blockade in **POOR WHITE**, his fifth novel that sorts the pieces and glimpses of a wandering youth. And the fiery, young, angry Erskine Caldwell in his epic piece **SACRILEGE OF ALLEN KENT** published by a small Maine print shop in 1933. Man alienated from society. America got fat and rich from resources and war. The true element, the communication from and with man to man became a hardening process. The stickball games are gone, the crap games in the schoolyard, the bonfires in the lot, mickey parties, lost orgies, even the baseball players lost their fire. O fat, primitive America. I blow fire up your asshole. Selby's **TRA-LA-LA** done shook 'em up, done blew a wig off a cat in London too. Bukowski in the dregs of L.A. blowing sounds for all of us. Let his voices be heard across the sands and deserts of this nation. Too much commercial bullshit. Too many face jobs, and nose jobs and clowns. A firebug dark German sleeps on a couch in the next room, writes all over the world turning people on. The doing and the deed is the revolution. Like the late sun breaking through clouds, red are the buildings, black are the walls. But the fucking sun lives on, comes after the night and blows our minds, yellow! Praise the original mind that breathes fresh air. Piss on despair, do ya hear. Adios, Baudelaire, firebug of my mind, longshots come home after a long ride!

   April 1968
   New York City

Micheline with poet Jack Hirschman, author of numerous books including **Black Alephs***,* **Lyripol***, and* **Endless Threshold***, on 16th Street, San Francisco, August 1992.*

Photo of unknown girl with parasol that Micheline purchased at a flea market. The photo hung in Micheline's storage space at 84 Sycamore Street, San Francisco.

RED HAIRED GODDESS

She is a poet Maria

a tall slim goddess

with earth in her thighs

Christ in the sky Maria

She is a poet

who danced in the streets

A goddess of love

part of the sun

with earth in her thighs

Maria

She loved all the poets

and wept by the grass

with wild red hair

Maria

From the unpublished manuscript:
Notes of the Lost Cities (1955-1962)

FRAGMENT

catastrophies
The light of nostrils forged with rain
wanderer
poet
sunlight of the brow
blind maidens
virgins of a dream
cutting the night
steam shovel of the world
Bleak
parasite
orphan
ragamuffin
costumes of despair
O World!
I shoot my stars
above your shallow grave
and bend the night
triumphant in my gaze
A lover's wish
more love upon the world
The dusk turns red and yellow
Fuck the Lies
We triumph with our eyes!

        January 22, 1969

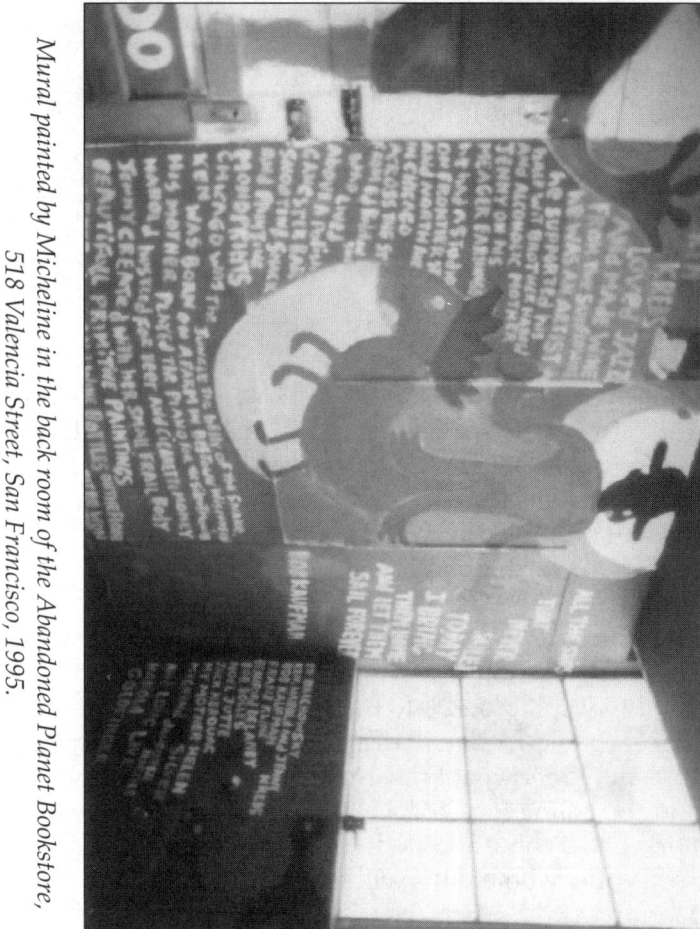

Mural painted by Micheline in the back room of the Abandoned Planet Bookstore, 518 Valencia Street, San Francisco, 1995.

© Photo by Scott Harrison

SHUFFLING THE DECK

Giant dirigibles float over my city
Sharks teeth bite at the poor
I look West to Harlem
East to the South Bronx
North to Queens
and South to Williamsburg
The Brooklyn Bridge
and the statue with the lady pissing
Children play in windows
and ancient Hebrews are too old to dream
The rattle of the snake is with the smoke of industry
Old railroad cars shuffle in the wind
In the asylums the druggist won his war
Bridges crumbled with old racing forms
In the junkyard gravestones of history
Let the darkness come
The stars will shine tonight
Tomorrow the dentist will pull my rotten teeth
and I will spit blood into the spittoons
The same old faces will drag themselves into bars
It seems America got too greedy
and the young look old
Spring will come and melt the snow of time
Seeds of newborn sons will howl
Eternity
Cities
Old wounds
and wars
Go shuffle the deck and the bitch queen
pulls down her pants and laughs at it all

      1990
      Brooklyn, NY

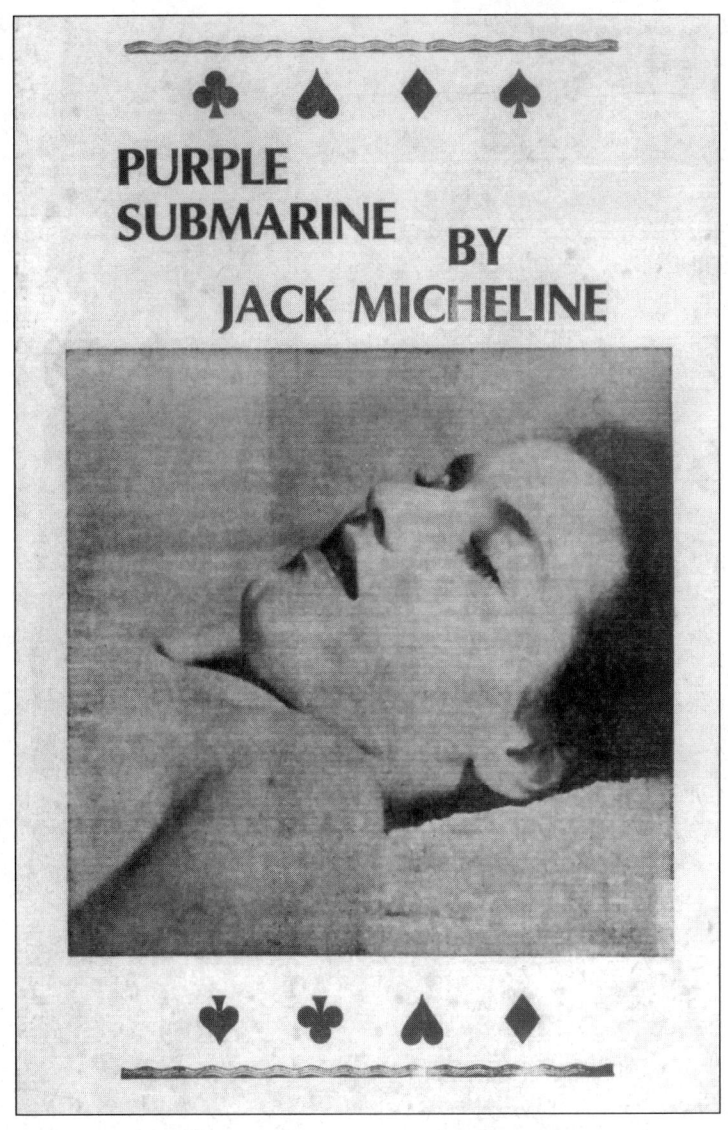

*Cover of Micheline's book **Purple Submarine** published by Kaye McDonough's Greenlight Press in 1976 in an edition of 530 copies.*

"Federico Garcia Lorca," 1976. Gouache on paper, 31 1/2" x 22".

BLACK DAY IN SPAIN
In memory of Federico Garcia Lorca

That day in Granada
The trees bent through

The gypsies lost their eyes
They came and took you

The sky was dark
They blindfolded your eyes

They tried to cover your eyes, Garcia
Against a black wall a flower grew

They shivered and fired
And the soil of Spain received you

       1963
       Altea, Spain

THE BALLAD OF JIMMY NELSON

Jimmy Nelson
was born
in a Tennessee
shack
born black
in a
Tennessee
shack
came to
Chicago
two years
ago
worked
as
a
porter
at
Montgomery
Ward
His body
was found
on Sagamon St.
a knife
in his gut
and a scar
on his face
Jimmy Nelson
lies dead

on Sagamon St.
twenty six
years
from
his birth
his girl
friends
still
echo
his
name
every night
Jimmy Nelson
Jimmy Nelson
where
are
you
Jimmy
Nelson

      1956
      Chicago, IL

      From the unpublished manuscript:
      Notes of the Lost Cities (1955-1962)

THE STREETS ARE YOURS BOBBY BOLLES

A letter told me you were gone
Wild child of the city
Irish son of the Brooklyn Ghetto
You came into Manhattan
Short guy with quick steps
Bright eyes and a hearty laugh
You sculpted on steel
Your figures of fire and light
Across Broome Street
From the dust of St. Adrian's Bar
The girls are dancing now
Your acetylene torch
Lighting up the night sky
Son of New York
The streets are yours Bobby Bolles

       October 10, 1989
       San Francisco, CA

BLUES FOR A BLONDE

Tell me baby
why you cry so much
Tell me baby
why you cry so much
words seem so gone
into the night
all we can say
the music goes on and on
all we can say
the music goes on and on
ain't what you done
ain't where you been
you got it now
it's always been
you could dance all night
and let the water roll
words ain't got it and never did
words ain't got it and never did

Prolouge To My Reading

My name is Jack Micheline
I am a Irish,gypsy, Pomanian Jewish Anarchist
born in the Bronx and a friend of the indians
Ive taken a dislike for publishers ,art galleries
and museums and the life style of poets, painters
and musicans. The reason I'm in Denver because I
showed up here. I have just putting together a
book for Howling Dog Press called The "Primer
of Self Liberation". My influences are Edgar Allan
Poe, Walt Whitman, Jack London, Baudelaire
Frederico Garcia Lorca, Franz Kline, James T FARRE
LL.Murrorvsky, Coltrane and Charles Mills.
among others. I Think art is a spiritual gift
not a commodity, Now I presume you know more about
me than myself, Shake the persons hand next to
you, Or kiss her knee whatever you perfer.
there is nothing wrong being friendly and
possitive, for I am at your service. and do not
be shocked if I blow your minds, For that is my
business, to shake the tree and kiss the Birdy
Pleasant Dreams...

                            Jack Micheline

Introductory remarks prepared by Micheline for a reading in Denver, Colorado, 1984. The book, Primer to Self-Liberation, *was never published, although three lithographed poem broadsides from the project were printed in late 1985.*

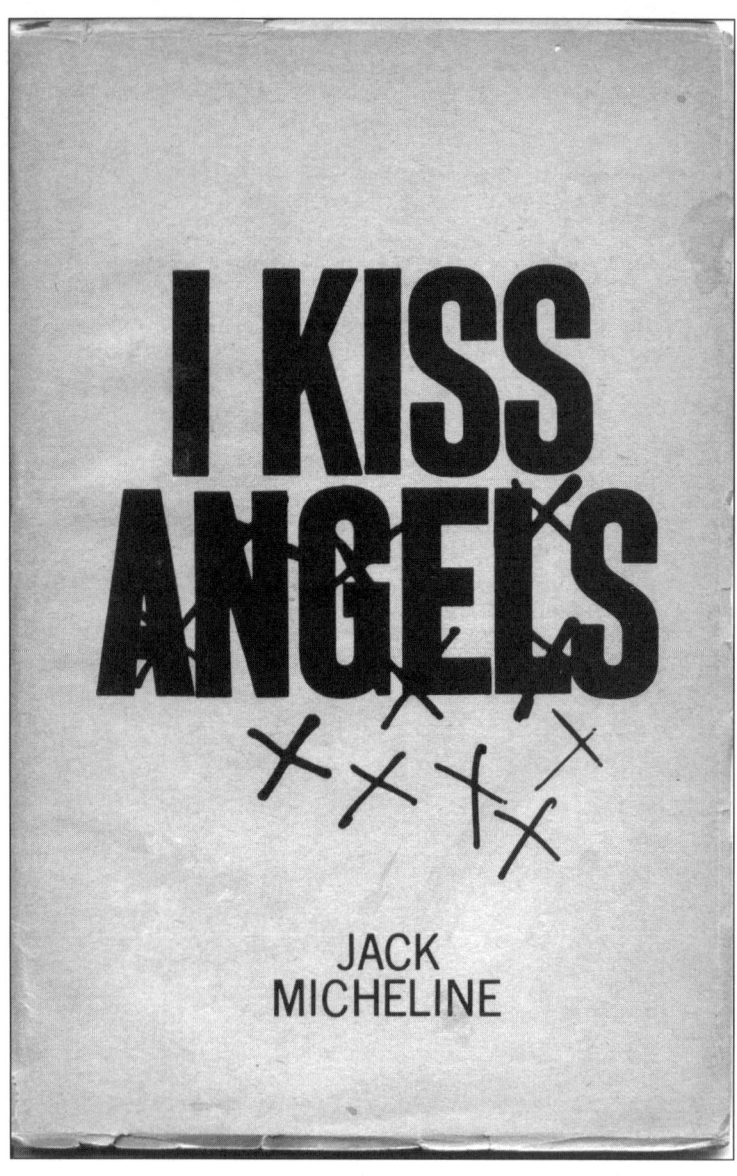

Cover of Micheline's second book, **I Kiss Angels**, edited by Jay Socin and published by Interim Books in New York City, in 1962, in an edition of 500 copies. The cover was designed by David Deutsch.

JENNY LEE

you never had a chance
   standing on a corner
      in the belly of Harlem
         and the horns were blowing crazy   jenny lee

shaking as a monkey has his way
   your veins bulged like rivers
      mad dogs are always biting
         the needle hard as iron   jenny lee

you had to make a dollar
   hustling in the street
      always voices in the rooms
         voices in your brain   jenny lee

you were fifteen when you started
   just earth and dogs and saliva cum
      hard rock
         black cat
            red bird   jenny lee

you never had a chance jenny lee
   scream and shake and vomit green
      the horns are always blowing

your guts cut out at twenty
   no black Jesus on a cross of neon
      preachers still wailing
         blue balls on the corner   jenny lee

you're born and you die
   no sweet ride for you baby
      the monkeys always jumpin
         all the faces of the angels

no more walking easter sunday
   no more turkey trimmings baby
      no more five star, rot gut sour whiskey   jenny lee

a sky full of flowers
  a yellow moon for you
    jenny died on the corner
      where all the voices were
        the horns were blowing crazy
          a siren wailed that night
            your body wrapped in flowers
              in the gutters of the sky
                out in the open
                  out in the street
                      heaven in your eyes   jenny lee

                Winter 1959
                Harlem

BACK OF TOWN BLUES

Rusted drain pipes
reached high above buildings
children ran after each other
women looked out windows
with bored faces
liquor stores and saloons
did a roaring business
I got that back of town blues
in back alleys cars and cats
and washline rainbows
waved back and forth
Negro mothers walked fat
in a tired lazy stroll
Back of town blues
was all over faces
Store front churches
sang loud with sorrow
gospel saviours
went to heaven
with the wretched poor
I got that back of town blues
Chariots blew their horns for Sadie
I got that back of town blues
Jimmy got drunk
on fire water and booze
just walking around with that
back of town blues

        Summer 1958
        San Francisco, CA

168   SIXTY-SEVEN POEMS FOR DOWNTRODDEN SAINTS

Micheline writing poetry on the side of a Southern Pacific railroad car, 1986.

ETERNITY

The Early Dawn of Warren Ohio in Eternity
Peter Orlovsky Sixteen in Eternity
Wordslinger Ray in Eternity
Harold Norse in Venice of Eternity
Charlie Bukowski's Eyes in Eternity
His Early Poems in Eternity
Odetta's Smile in Eternity
The Open Void and the Prairies of Kansas in Eternity
Tallahassee, Shreveport, New Orleans, Detroit,
San Francisco, New York, Chicago, All in Eternity
Malcolm Raphael, Bob Blossom, Jimmy Baldwin
His Eyes in Eternity
Lucien in Eternity, Richie, Adrian, Betty Sue, Mirianne
Patricia, My Son Vinny in Eternity
The Buildings of Downtown New York in Eternity
The Streets of Red Hook and South Brooklyn, Staten Island
East 87th Street by the Waters of Eternity
Altea Spain in Eternity
Serge Challoff His Wife and Sandra Young in Eternity
The Thighs of Young Women in Eternity
The Streets of Paris All in My Mind of Eternity
    Mobile
        Memphis
            Monterey
                Occalula
                    Oshkosh in the Dusk of Eternity
Jerry Kemstra of Potrero Hill in Eternity
The Railroad Yards of Cicero
Gleaming in the Night of Eternity
Bob Bowden on the Spoon River of Eternity
The Brooklyn Bridge Waving in Eternity
Thieves Lighting the Stairway to Eternity
Ed Balchowsky Singing Old Spanish War Songs

On the Rooftops of Eternity
His One Arm in Eternity
Harold Goldfinger Raving in Eternity
Rick Librizzi Jumping Trains in Eternity
The Face of Franz Kline Forever in Eternity
The Wind and Railroad Trains in Eternity
Sweet Charlie Mingus in Eternity
Puerto Rican LoLo, Fernando Vega, Tony Fruscella
Blowing in Eternity
Allen Ginsberg's Heart in Eternity
Harold Anton, Charles Mills, and Tom Keats
Soaring in Eternity
Chicago in Eternity
Wandering in the Wilderness of Eternity
Jack Kerouac Riding the Ole Angel Midnight
His Hands Outstretched
His Face Against the Sky
Embracing the Cold Shivering Cities
Caw-
Caw-
Caw-
Caw- in Eternity

    November 5, 1971
    New York City
    (This version edited 1996)

A POET CAN BE A SHOEMAKER

Don't expect anyone to

Understand to blow

A kiss in a cold night

A poet can be a shoemaker

A waitress who never

Wrote a line

A poet could be the

Invisible man

>From a letter to Ben Gulyas
>January 5, 1989

REQUIEM

Two bridges

And the empire state

I caught the

Eyeballs of a city

In the gypsy

Mother of us all

Wrecked lives

On a dark street

Near dusk

On a Woodside

Train station

Death is the side

Of darkness

And the peace

        May 3, 1982
        Train Station, 6 a.m.
        Woodside, New York

JACK MICHELINE

© Photo by Fred W. McDarrah

Micheline, Frank O'Hara (b. 1926, Baltimore, MD — d. 1966, Fire Island, NY), author of **A City Winter, and Other Poems**, **Meditations In An Emergency**, and **Lunch Poems**; Barbara Guest, author of **Herself Defined, The Poet H.D. and her World**, and **Seeking Air**; Allan Kaplan, and Abram Schlemowitz, among others, at the closing of the original Cedar Tavern, March 30, 1963, New York City.

BEAUFORD DELANEY IN PARIS 1964

In a poor section of Paris
I took off my shoes
before I entered his studio
A stocky frail man
With a black moon face
We went to the grocer to buy vegetables
he cooked me a delicious meal
his studio was clean as a whistle
he went into his closet and took out
one painting after the other, he showed me
one beautiful painting after another
It was like entering a rare chapel
              a unique mosque
                  a temple of the sublime
                      a house of spiritual endeavor
                  a high rising of the light
                a deep religious experience
            a moment never to be forgotten
one by one he showed me his paintings
one shot across the moon
one shot against the darkness of the night
one shot for a wild-eyed artist
one shot for man and mankind
one shot for genius
one shot for Aurora Borealis
one shot for the children of time
Long Live Beauford Delaney
one shot for the world

       1991
       San Francisco, CA

*Beauford Delaney, painter (b. 1901, Knoxville, TN —
d. 1979, Paris, France). In 1964 Micheline visited
Delaney at his Rue Vercingetorix studio in Paris.*

UNTITLED

1

I hear the ghosts of

Rummies shuffling in the dark

And the flying hoofs

In the stretches of time

2

Tom Halley's wife bled in the gutter

Franz Kline's wife went insane

The bottle was the hero

Nothing more

3

John Richardson the poet wasn't strong

So he died alone

Mother of the thirsty blood

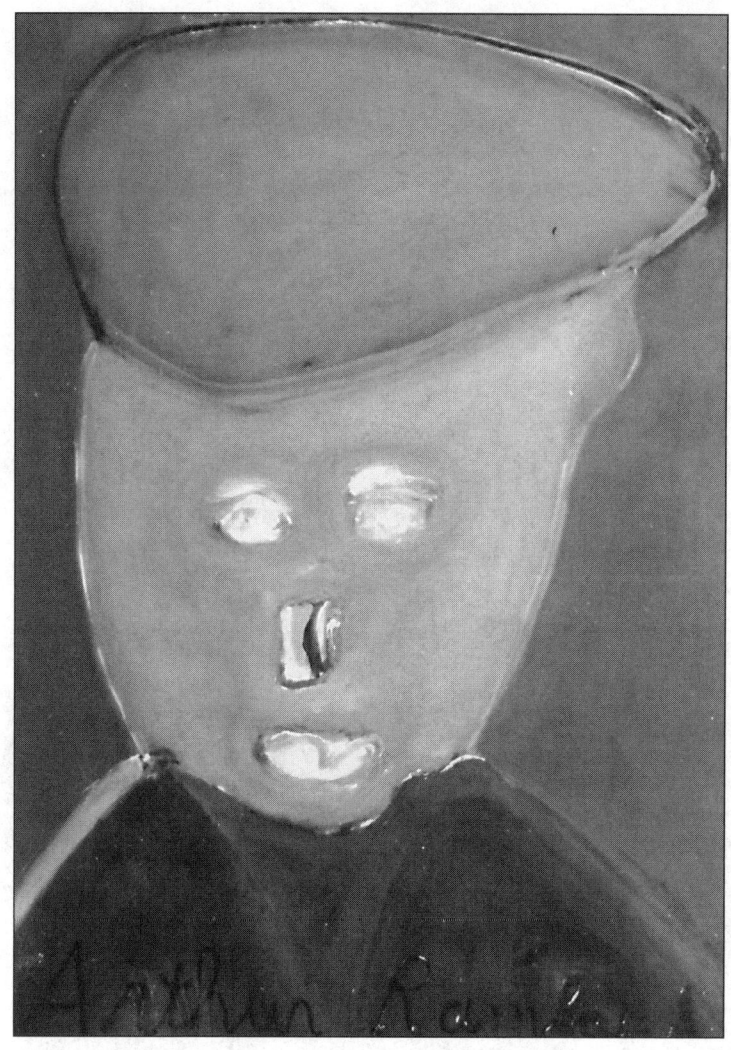

"Arthur Rimbaud," 1976. Gouache on paper, 29 1/2" x 21 1/4".

Untitled, 1962. Ink and wash on paper, 23 ½" × 18".

SOULS
*A dirge in memory of my grandfather
Louis Silver Lipinsky*

I will never forget you grandfather Louie
white hair covering your head
as you told children fairy tales
your white beard flowing
with the psalms of David in your hand
you chose to wander
corpses white around you Louie
where there was no light
only in the wisdom of men
you were somewhere searching
hearing the chants of babies
I could not bear to see you buried
wandering in the slums of wild children
you hear me now
the blind spoke to you with their eyes
sometimes life is bitter than the passing
solemn only in a sky of flowers
solemn only in a moon with many eyes
voices of the shallow calling

condemned you loafer, bum

you wandered storyteller, fisherman

without trial or jury

the poison tongues of narrow men

we should not speak

you said that men had faces light and dark

a tailor in the stitches of his life

a tailor in a prison of his soul

so we chose the open air

it is the desert walked by unknown feet

it is the song of whistling birds

it is the blowing wind of trees

it is the vision of the flutes

it is man that tortures man

it is the whip of jealous men

it is the madness of my youth

it is the scars of disbelief

it is the desert of our souls

so I ran to unknown Gods to find a haven

the years that color never showed

it was the years of endless groping

a child searching for a land that never was

it was always black and muddy somewhere else

it was the cries of other men

it was the shouting and the burning of our youth

it is the mountain of the victims of mankind

it is out of darkness comes the light

it is out of tears that scars did fall

it is love that filtered through my tortured soul

I write this poem on Yom Kippur to you

the face of wandering men across your soul

machinery is grinding flesh of men

no ceremony to glorify the dead

only the earth that covers you

only the stars

out of the darkness comes this poem

out of the madness of this world

the Gods have blessed me with a flower

we are evil as a flower

it is the blindness I have seen

it is the feet of marching men

it is the death I have seen

it is the envy I have seen

it is the daggers in the smiles of the mind

it is the stone that covers us

it is the sounds of marching feet

it is the talk gone endless to its nowhere

it is the twisted childhood

it is the mother's tender clutch

that sometimes smothers

it is the sun that luminates all darkness

is is life twisted by our proudness

it is the laugh of the not so saintly tortures

it is the courtroom full of lawyers

it is the children born in chains

it is the anger taken away

it is the suck of all the money

it is the wobbly feet we bring to manhood

it is the look of earthy faces

it is the silence tearing at our throats

it is the power of nothingness

it is the fear driven inward

it is the mirror we never look into

it is the preacher

it is the river

it is the fire

it is the wanderer searching for his soul

it is the very steel invisible

it is the tower of Babel

it is the poet of the streets

it is Sherwood

it is Mahatma

it is the cat that licked my nose

it is the vision unconquered

it is D. H. Lawrence

it is Dostoevski

it is the unknown

it is the invisible

it is life that never faded

it is darkness

it is the vision of the flutes

it is the pillars of the sky

it is destiny

it is fate

it is America out of the fog

it is all

it is all of us

it is the eyes

it is the strangers

it is the lonely hitchhiker

it is the songs unsung

it is the concerto of our brain

it is life itself

it is the dead

it is the dying

it is the users

it is the fist of power

it is the face of the conjurers

it is the parades that swallow the young

it is the bandwagon

it is not out there

it is you

it is the light here in darkness

it is life itself

it is love to all the virgins

it is the cat that licked my nose

it is the vision of the flutes

it is the hand outstretched in darkness

it is the rain

it is the wheat of golden sunsets

it is the million empty houses

it is the voices

it is the rooms

it is the knife

it is the unknowing

it is the killing

it is the rape

it is the flowers

it is faith taken from us

it is the doubt

it is all the mountains

it is the children

it is the streets of drunken madness

burning in our souls

it is judgment turned against us

it is the face of grandfather Louie

it is America out of the fog

it is the vision of the flutes

it is Kol Nidre

it is the seeds left scattered

it is the nod of all the strangers

it is the long sound unanswered

it is grandfather Louie

I know you smile now

I could not bear to see you buried

wandering in the slums of wild children

faces of wandering men across your soul

no ceremony to glorify the dead

only the earth that covers you

only the stars

    September 1957
    Brooklyn, NY

    Written on a holy vision of the flutes
    on Yom Kippur the night of Kol Nidre

*Micheline at the corner of Valencia and 16th Street,
San Francisco, March 1992.*

BEAT NO CHASER
WESTCOAST BEATS CONVERGE
Friday, August 22
8pm
presented by (Sic) Random Vice & Verse
GLAXA STUDIOS 3707 SUNSET Blvd. in Silverlake
An evening of spoken word
PHILOMENE LONG
JACK $6.00
MICHELINE
FRANK T. RIOS
TONY SCIBELLA
JOHN THOMAS
HOSTED BY S.A. GRIFFIN

Flyer designed by Andy Takakjian advertising a spoken word event featuring members of the Venice Beach Beat scene of the late 1960s and early 1970s, produced by Rafael F.J. Alvarado and S.A. Griffin, for the magazine (Sic) Vice & Verse, at Glaxa Studios in Los Angeles, August 22, 1997.

MAKE YOUR COLOR IN THE SKY

Make a mark
With your finger
Like a heartbeat on a wall
Like the wind
Make your mark
With a pencil
A crayon
A piece of chalk
Footsteps on concrete
In a prison
In a madhouse
Make a mark
With your finger
A crayon
A piece of chalk
Make another mark
Like the wind
On a subway platform
Footsteps on concrete
In a prison
In a madhouse
Make your color
In the sky
Like a heartbeat
In the night
A finger moves
Like the wind
Make your mark
With your eyes

*Cover of Micheline's book **Skinny Dynamite**, translated into German by Carl Weissner, and published by Maro Verlag in West Germany in March 1979. The cover photo of Micheline is by Ed Buryn, and the cover collage design is by Walter Hartmann. The book contained four stories not included in the American edition which was published the following year.*

PERSONAL

U.S.A.

Well Built Buxom

Mature Positive

Woman 40 — 60 Sought

By Romantic Relocatable

Man 64   5'11"   185 lbs

Good Looking Intelligent

Retired Artist

Needs Big Woman To

Love Photo Phone

Will Answer All

Marriage Possible

    1994
    San Francisco

192 SIXTY-SEVEN POEMS FOR DOWNTRODDEN SAINTS

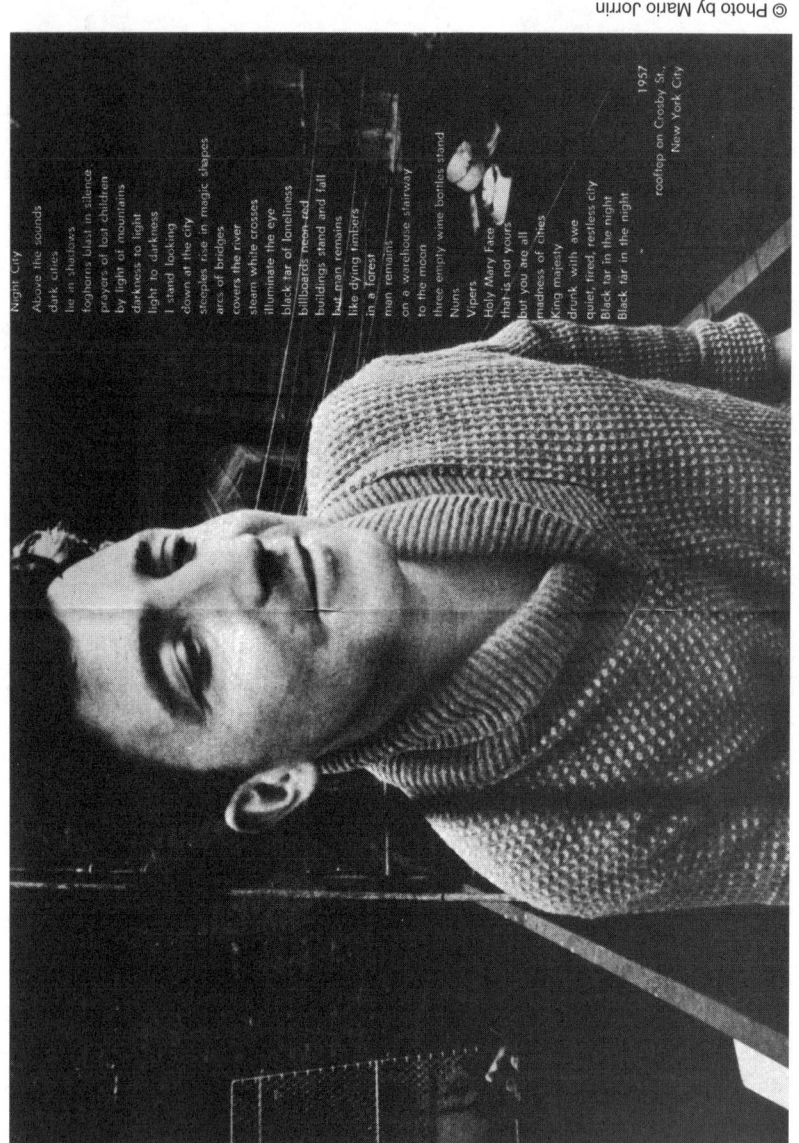

© Photo by Mario Jorrin

Photo which appeared in Micheline's second book, *I Kiss Angels*, showing Micheline on an apartment rooftop in New York City, c. 1962. The photo originally appeared as a two-page spread with the poem "Night City" which appears on page 80 of this book.

POEM

To capture the feeling

To feel its pulse

To see the stream has been muddied

I am busy reshaping the stars

I cannot be bothered with your

Earthly pleasures

All these rantings and ravings

Have nothing to do with poetry

Have nothing to do with magic

Only the ears of butterflies

And birds

And the delicate moths

Matter

Let the Angels in

Let them into this Market

Now

Feel, see, and breathe

>February 25, 1998
>San Francisco

SAN FRANCISCO'S
JACK MICHELINE
POET PAINTER

ART WORKS
ON THE WALL

CITY LIGHTS BOOKS
261 COLUMBUS

NOV 1 THRU DEC 31
'86

Dwarfs, Ships, Monks, and Funny People:

Works of Jack Micheline

Thursday
September 29th, 1988

Copperfield's Books
153 Kentucky Street
Petaluma, California 94952

Artist's Reception
&
Jazz Music

7pm-9pm
Thursday
September 29th, 1988

Micheline looking for poems in his storage space at 84 Sycamore Street in San Francisco, c. 1995.

I WINK AT THE GRAVEYARDS IN QUEENS

I'm excited

I'm always excited

A smile

A handshake

A slap on the back

A kiss

I'm dancing in the street

I wink at the graveyards in Queens

New York I'm gonna beat your ass

I'm gonna lick your ass

Beat death

Beat death

Beat death

Beat death

Beat death

    November 3, 1978

BOWERY BLACK

Puke your guts near the bowery black
Birds will sing a song for you
Grey beard men are invisible men
Lick your chops on a bugler's Roll
With dirty shirt Mack at your heels
Singing the Blues as the trucks roll by
City wakes up in a haze of time
Wine of the night to a fairy moon
An American dream in holy socks
Jehovah-God is a rummy song
By Kingdom hall steps in the night
Butchers and Bakers and fruit pedlar Sam
Pick up the empties for half a square meal
Sleep on the benches of Allen St. Jive
There's Salvation on Sweet Charlie's face
Mad Hank is Christ in his grave
Piles of chicken hearts in pussy house square
Clothesline a ship on the rolling sea
Mark your time in a scoreboard night
City wakes up to a Lion's Roar
With the Diesel Engine trucks in the sky
Caesar, Napoleon, Christ in Concrete
Church bells sing the priests' good tune
Statutes are green in the snakes of the moon
Truck driver's grin of a whorehouse dream
Teeth of the tiger has taken its toll
Moon is dead
George is gone
I'm on my way in a pillow of clouds
Feathers of Pigeons
Bald men of Rome
Sleeping in the doorway bunks
Your King and Queen of Soul and Spit
Give me a night in the cool breeze dawn
The crowd is roarin' for a bloody fight

While the engines roar to the bleeding Sun
Blind Man Sweeny
Black Duke's dream
faces in buses
horn blowin' freak
in the hammock of my brain
of a madman's dawn
as the wobblies
walk in the Sun

   c. 1957

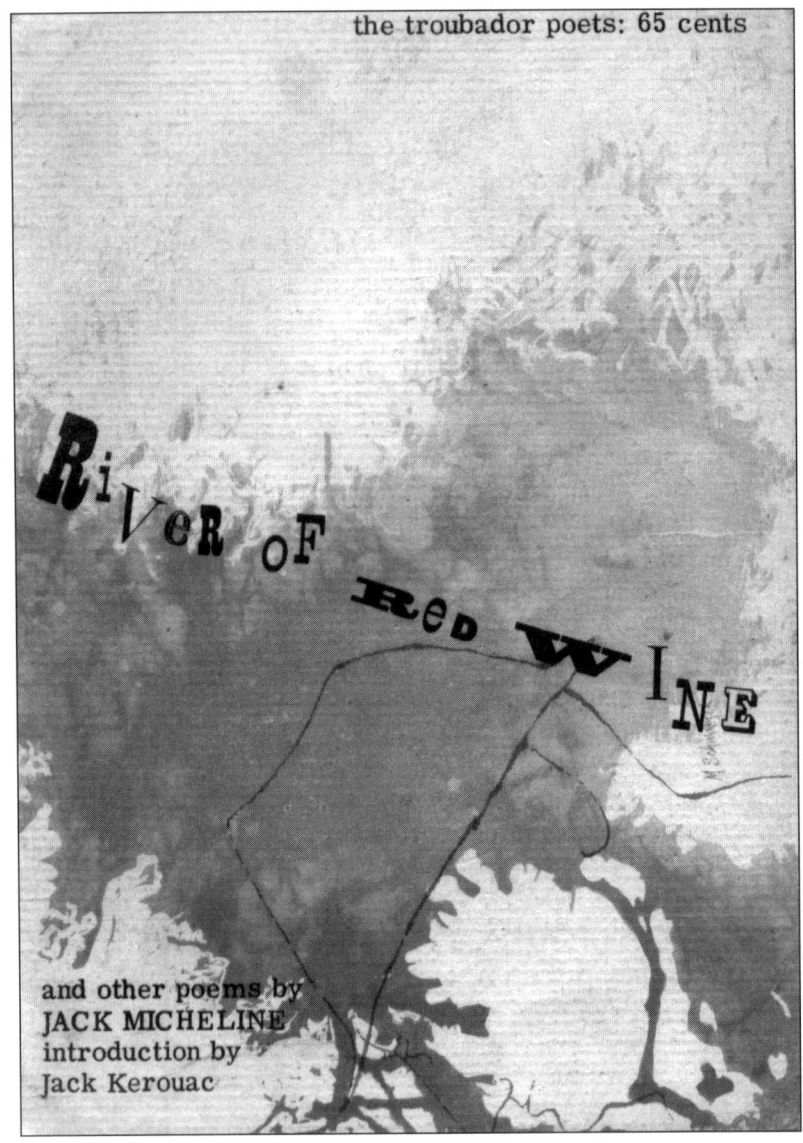

Cover of Micheline's first book, **River of Red Wine**, edited by Robert Grantham and published by Brayton Harris' Troubador Press in New York City, in 1958. The cover was designed by Marlene Schwanzel.

OUTSIDE GARY

In 1956 I lay dead on a highway outside Gary

With an empty wine bottle in one hand

And poems scrawled in the other

Thinking of how the corpses of six million Jews

Lie rotting in the soil of Europe

And of how in America

Everyone goes shopping in a supermarket

Do you know

They remaindered Lorca for 69 cents

And the bookseller cried he lost money

How blind I was

How wrong I was

How child I was

I feel the anguish of man in the chaos of this world

Send me flowers

    1961
    New York City

BEAT THE DRUM FOR ME NICKY

With her short hands
And wide grin
My Grand daughter Nicole
Beats the drum For me
She sits at her small desk
And draws her dreams
Makes butterflies and horsies
From the Playdough machine
She has a dog named Sangie
A daddy named Vince
A Moma called Sheri
And a grandma Pat
And once in a while
an old Man comes around
And his name — is Grandpa Jack
Beat the drum For Me Nicky
Beat A Monkey with A stick
When the Moon is Funny
And the Moon is high
Once in a while
an Old MAN comes by
And his Name is Grandpa Jack
Beat the drum for me Nicky
Beat the drum For ME

1997

*Micheline's granddaughter Nicole Solai Silvaer
(b. January 31, 1995, Tucson, AZ).*

Painting of Chuck Gonzalez, leader of the band Lessick's Kid of Bloomington, Indiana, 1997. Mixed media on paper, 11" x 8 1/2". Gonzalez collaborated with Micheline on many songs during the late summer of 1997, including the arrangement and music for "Old Maid," "A Long Long Time," and "Sweet Sue, Pennsylvania," which was a reworking of Micheline's song, "Just Ramble On." Micheline called the 612 N. Lincoln Street house Gonzalez lived in "The Jelly Jam Factory."

SWEET SUE, PENNSYLVANIA *(a song)*

There's flowers in the sky
There's a gleam in her eye
There's a road down the street
There's a look in her eye
There's a time to be born
And a time to die
There's a cross on The Hill
There's Buffalo Bill

Sweet Sue, Pennsylvania
Texas prairie grass
California, California

There's the apple man
And the junk man too
And the iceman comes
With the milkman train
Cows in the field
And the river flowing wide
There's a woman by my side
She's the sun and the sky

Sweet Sue, Pennsylvania
Texas prairie grass
California, California

There's a strawberry patch
And the jasmine tree
There's children singing songs
And the bumble bee
I'm a wandering man
I'm a minstrel man
There's a gleam in my eye
I'm going to smile when I die

Sweet Sue, Pennsylvania
Texas prairie grass
California, California

      August 26, 1997
      The Jelly Jam Factory
      Bloomington, Indiana

Micheline with his friend of 37 years, Abstract Expressionist painter Tom Schultz, at the Adobe Bookshop, San Francisco, 1992.

A LONG LONG TIME *(a song)*

I've been out of my mind
Riding a train
Singing my song
I've been hitchin' a ride
Walking the streets
And blowing my sound

For a long long time
I've been out of my mind
A long long time
I've been out of my mind

The streets been my home
In the park there are trees
The sky is my pillow
Birds in the air
They fly everywhere
And clouds for a dream

For a long long time
I've been out of my mind
A long long time
I've been out of my mind

This trip I've been on
Moving around
From town to town
The children smile
As I pass them by
I'm a crazy vagabond

For a long long time
I've been out of my mind
A long long time
I've been out of my mind
I've been out of my mind
I've been out of my mind
For a long time

    c. 1970
    (This song arranged 1997)

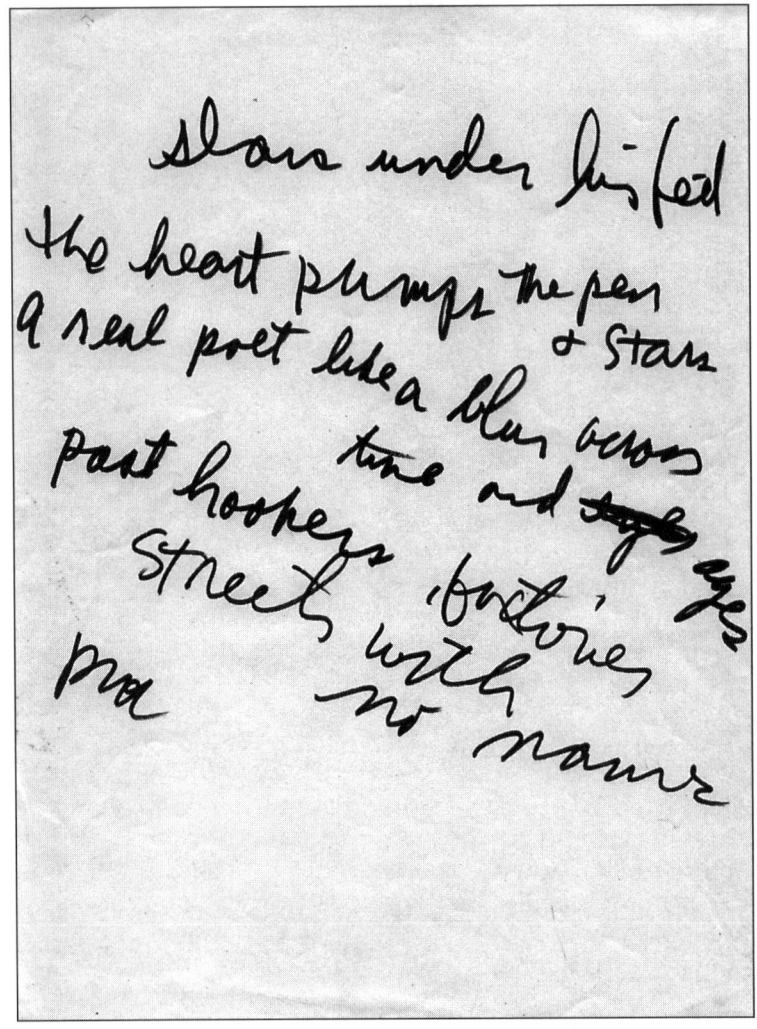

An undated handwritten poem fragment given to editor Matt Gonzalez by Micheline two days before his death for inclusion in the revised edition of **Sixty-seven Poems for Downtrodden Saints**. *It reads: "Stars under his feet/The heart pumps the pen and stars/A real poet like a blur across/Time and ages/Past hookers, factories/Streets with no names..."*

OUT OF THE RAINS

Out of the rains
And mud of cities
Walking in a fog
On subway platforms
In Harlem and Brooklyn and Queens
I see the faces of children
Staring at me
And I want to run from the city
Past freights
And ships
And buildings that scrape the sky
I want to race down streets
Dreaming of mountains and Spanish girls
I am a poet
I stare at the ground to see if I am bleeding

    1966
    New York City

Untitled, 1978. Gouache on paper, 30" x 22".

HISTORY IS BEAUTIFUL

I am Vachel Lindsay

I am Charles Baudelaire

I am Arthur Rimbaud

I am Walt Whitman

I am Federico Garcia Lorca

I am Guillaume Apollinaire

I am Francois Villon

I am Bob Kaufman

I am Langston Hughes

I am Vladimir Mayakovsky

I am Jack Micheline

>   1997
>   San Francisco

Micheline with $5,600 he won on a trifecta bet at the Aquaduct Racetrack in Queens, New York. Photo taken in photographer Ramon Muxter's studio on Spring Street, New York City, 1976.

Afterword

The poems in this volume were taken from previously published and unpublished books, pamphlets, broadsides, scraps of paper, napkins, postcards, brown paper bags, torn book covers, letters, notebooks, racing forms, and poem paintings. Micheline provided full access to his archives, which consists of material not included in The Bancroft Library, now stored in a locker on Page Street in San Francisco. In some cases, efforts to salvage poems found in the over fifty suitcases and trunks were unsuccessful as Micheline's handwriting was so bad, or paper had been damaged by water or years of storage, that neither of us could make out entire lines of his writing. Other poems were rescued and have managed to find their way into this collection. Emphasis has been placed on publishing poems never before collected in Micheline's previous books. In order to present a literary portrait of Micheline it was necessary to complement the poems found in his locker with previously published work that has become synonymous with his name and well-known through his public readings and bootleg audio recordings. This is a noteworthy publication as it covers Micheline's entire career and is the largest collection published by him in over twenty years.

Commenting on poetic inspiration, Micheline once said that poetry comes from his head, his heart, his cock, his toes, that it is a light that rips him bare. That the poems in this collection convey genuine sentiments will be evident. It is inevitable, however, that some readers will object to certain poems because they are vulgar or offensive in some other manner. These poems must be read in their context, for no poem in this collection is meant to cause offense to anyone. This collection is full of laughter, the affirmation of life, love, and sometimes despair. The poems, some of which are over forty years old, come from different periods in our nation's history and in the life of the poet. No matter what the individual conclusion of the reader, they are vintage Micheline, full of hustlers, rooming houses, mattresses, and evictions. These poems are the life he has known.

Anyone interested in more biographical information on Micheline or in critical essays reviewing his career should consult the following publications, some of which, regrettably, contain minor errors:

Josh Gosciak, "'Beat' Poetry in the Seventies, an Interview with Jack Micheline," *Contact II*, vol. 2, no. 11 (Nov.-Dec. 1978), pp. 32-35, eds. Maurice Kenny and J.G. Gosciak.

Dwight Chapin, "The Joy of Painting," *San Francisco Examiner*, (March 20, 1981), D1.

Jack Micheline, "Jack Micheline Enjoys Jack Kerouac Conference Held by Naropa in Boulder," *Daily Planet International* (September 2, 1982).

Jack Micheline, "I Ain't No Poet, I Fly with the Angels, Imaginary Interview with Jack Micheline," *New Blood*, no. 8 (November 1982), pp. 28-29, ed. Niko Murray.

Gerald Nicosia, "Jack Micheline," DICTIONARY OF LITERARY BIOGRAPHY, VOLUME 16: THE BEATS: LITERARY BOHEMIANS IN POSTWAR AMERICA (Detroit, Michigan: Gale Research Co., 1983) pp. 410-415.

Joel Scherzer and Tony Moffeit, "Selling Light on Street Corners, an Interview with *a cappella* Singer and Poet Jack Micheline," *The Bloomsbury Review*, (April 1985), pp. 19-21, ed. Robbie Rubinstein.

Neeli Cherkovski, "Jack Micheline at the SF Press Club," *Haight Ashbury Literary Journal*, vol. 2, no. 2 (1986), p. 13.

Joel Scherzer and Tony Moffeit, "An Interview with Jack Micheline," **WRITERS OUTSIDE THE MARGIN, AN ANTHOLOGY** (Sudbury, Massachusetts: Water Row Press, 1986), pp. 13-17, ed. Jeffrey H. Weinberg.

"Jack Micheline," **CONTEMPORARY AUTHORS**, vol. 122 (Detroit, Michigan: Gale Research Co., 1988), pp. 320-324, eds. Hal May and Susan M. Trosky; (includes an interview of Micheline by Jean W. Ross).

"Jack Micheline, Sad for an Unbrave World," *Beat Scene* (England), no. 9 (1990), p. 26.

 The "Acknowledgments" compiled for this book do not comprise a complete bibliography. I have merely given credit to prior Micheline collections and to whatever anthologies were available to me. I have credited Micheline's unpublished manuscript "Notes of the Lost Cities," separately, at the bottom of the poem where applicable. In my opinion it is a collection that more than any other unpublished Micheline collection I have seen, stands as its own volume, and therefore should receive that acknowledgement. Some of the poems in that manuscript have been previously published, including some I have selected for this volume, but the manuscript has never appeared in its entirety.
 Micheline has not been easy to work with, and anyone who knows him will know exactly what I am talking about. In many cases he denied writing a poem I had discovered among his papers, insisting that he see the original before acknowledging authorship. In other instances he wanted poems destroyed that he later decided he liked quite a bit.

And on a few occasions he did not want poems included in this collection because they were too personal, or might be misunderstood. Often I think Micheline disliked or criticized a poem merely because I expressed satisfaction with it. Suffice it to say we both welcome this book's publication.

Wherever possible Micheline's original spelling of words has been retained, his desire to avoid apostrophes, his irregular syntax, his self-created sound-words, and his non-uniform capitalization, have been respected. Exceptions were made where typographical errors were plainly evident or where Micheline himself indicated prior publication errors. No change to any poem, however trivial, was made without his approval. Careful attention has been brought to this project. Any apparent mistakes in the text should be viewed as purposeful.

Finally, the title, SIXTY-SEVEN POEMS FOR DOWNTRODDEN SAINTS, is meant to commemorate Micheline's sixty-seventh birthday, which he celebrated November 6, 1996. It does not refer to the actual number of poems in this collection.

— Matt Gonzalez, *Editor*
February 14, 1997

Sixteen poems, one prose broadside, "The Land of the Savage," and the autobiographical "Mr Jack Micheline," have been added to the second edition, none of which have appeared in any of Micheline's previous books. Micheline reviewed each poem added to this collection before his death in February 1998, except for the two songs "Long Long Time" and "Sweet Sue, Pennsylvania" and the poem to his granddaughter "Beat the Drum for Me Nicky." The two songs were arranged by Charles Gonzalez and Micheline approved of the recorded versions. The poem to his granddaughter was found among his papers after his death. He is known to have read the poem at "Second Story" in Bloomington, Indiana, on August 30, 1997.

— M.G.
October 31, 1998

Acknowledgments

Micheline's Books:

"Poem to My Grandfather" and "Let's Sing a Song" previously appeared in RIVER OF RED WINE (New York: Troubador Press, 1958).

"The Dead Are Gone," "Everywhere I Go," "Night City," and "Jenny Lee" previously appeared in I KISS ANGELS (New York: Interim Books, 1962).

"Night City" previously appeared in STREET OF LOST FOOLS (Mastic, New York: Street Press, 1975).

"All People Are Enslaved," "Illumination," and "Streetcall New Orleans" previously appeared in POEMS OF DR INNISFREE (San Francisco: Beatitude Press, 1975).

"These Streets I Walk Upon," "Poem: I kiss the dead face of a Russian girl" (in different form), "Night City," "Blues Poem," "South Street Pier," "Jenny Lee," and "Back of Town Blues" previously appeared in YELLOW HORN (San Francisco: Golden Mountain Press, 1975).

"Poem to the Freaks," "Long After Midnight," "Jenny Lee," and "Back of Town Blues" previously appeared in LAST HOUSE IN AMERICA (San Francisco: Second Coming Press, 1976).

"Everywhere I Go" appeared on the record accompanying PURPLE SUBMARINE (San Francisco: Greenlight Press, 1976).

"Down by the Wild," "Poet of the Streets," "The Dead Are Gone," "Everywhere I Go," "These Streets I Walk Upon," "Poem to My Grandfather," "Poem: I kiss the dead face of a

Russian girl" (in different form), "Poem Written on a Hollywood Back Street Sunday Morning," "Night City," "Blues Poem," "Let's Sing A Song," "South Street Pier," "Streetcall New Orleans," "Black Day in Spain," "Jenny Lee," and "Back of Town Blues" previously appeared in NORTH OF MANHATTAN, COLLECTED POEMS, BALLADS AND SONGS: 1954-1975 (South San Francisco: ManRoot, 1976).

"Illumination," "Jenny Lee," and "Back of Town Blues" previously appeared in ACAPPELLA RABBI, A JACK MICHELINE SAMPLER (Pueblo, Colorado: Quick Books, 1986).

"Chasing Kerouac's Shadow" (under the title "Walking in Kerouac's Shadow") previously appeared in IMAGINARY CONVERSATION WITH JACK KEROUAC (Oakland: Zeitgeist Press, 1989).

"Beauty Is Everywhere Baudelaire" and "Hiding Places" previously appeared in OUTLAW OF THE LOWEST PLANET (Oakland: Zeitgeist Press, 1993).

"Eternity" previously appeared in an unedited version in ETERNITY & DANCING ON THE OTHER SIDE OF THE STREET (Stow, Ohio: Implosion Press, 1996).

"Souls" previously appeared in SOULS (San Francisco: Express Press, 1997).

"Blues for a Blonde" and "Souls" previously appeared in A DAGGER AT YOUR HEART (San Francisco: Midnight Special Edition, 1997).

Anthologies:

"To Be a Poet Is to Live and Die"and "Bowery Black" previously appeared in *Nomad*, (Spring 1959), pp. 10-13, eds. Donald Factor and Anthony Linick.

"All People are Enslaved" previously appeared in THE BEAT SCENE (New York: Corinth Books, 1960), ed. Elias Wilentz.

"Streetcall New Orleans" previously appeared in THE BEATS (Greenwich, Connecticut: Gold Medal Books, 1960), ed. Seymour Krim, and *The Outsider*, vol. 1, no. 2, (Summer 1962), pp. 94-96, eds. Jon and Louise Webb.

"Someday I'll Live Forever" previously appeared in *Cosmos* (England), no. 1 (1969), p. 5, eds. Steve MacDonogh and Michael Gray.

"Long After Midnight" previously appeared in *Second Coming*, vol. 2, no. 3 (1974) (special Bukowski edition), pp. 24-25, ed. A.D. Winnans, and in SECOND COMING ANTHOLOGY: TEN YEARS IN RETROSPECT (San Francisco: Second Coming Anthology, 1984), ed. A.D. Winans.

"Let's Sing a Song" and "Jenny Lee" previously appeared in DUSP (DENVER UNION OF STREET POETS) ANTHOLOGY (Denver, Colorado: S.E.A. Press, 1981), ed. Padraic Cooper.

"Eternity" previously appeared in an unedited version in *New Blood*, no. 8 (November 1982), p. 30, ed. Niko Murray.

"Rambling Jack" previously appeared in BEATITUDE 33, SILVER ANNIVERSARY (San Francisco: Beatitude, 1985), ed. Jeffrey Grossman.

"Chasing Kerouac's Shadow" previously appeared in STORIES AND POEMS FROM CLOSE TO HOME (Berkeley, California: Ortalda & Associates, 1986), ed. Floyd Salas, and under the title "Walking in Kerouac's Shadow" in WRITERS OUTSIDE THE MARGIN, AN ANTHOLOGY (Sudbury, Massachusetts: Water Row Press, 1986), ed. Jeffrey H. Weinberg.

"On Franz Kline" (taped by Kush), previously appeared in an unedited version in *Third Rail*, no. 8 (1987), p. 28, ed. Uri Hertz.

"Blues Poem" previously appeared in THE JAZZ POETRY ANTHOLOGY (Bloomington: Indiana University Press, 1991), eds. Sascha Feinstein and Yusef Komunyakaa.

"Sainthood Is for the Birds" previously appeared in *Art Crimes*, no. 11 (April 1991), p. 12, ed. Ben Gulyas.

"Poet of the Streets" previously appeared in THE PORTABLE BEAT READER (New York: Viking Penguin, 1992), ed. Ann Charters.

"A Poet Can Be a Shoemaker" previously appeared in *Split City*, (Fall 1992), p. 20, (special Micheline edition), eds. Ben Gulyas, Jim Lang and Mike Thomas.

"Hiding Places" previously appeared in THE ADOBE ANTHOLOGY (San Francisco: The Adobe Bookshop, 1993), ed. Claudia Lunstroth.

"Poem: I chose the whippoorwill" previously appeared in ARGONAUT, (Spring 1994), p. 313, ed. Warren Hinckle.

"Back of Town Blues" previously appeared in BEAT GENERATION, GLORY DAYS IN GREENWICH VILLAGE (New York: Schirmer Books, 1996), eds. Fred W. and Gloria S. McDarrah.

"Out of the Rains" and "Poem: To capture the feeling," previously appeared in the obituary by Eric Brazil, "Jack Micheline, Poet, Painter, Free Spirit," *San Francisco Examiner*, March 1, 1998, p. D-8.

"Outside Gary," "Poem: To capture the feeling," "Poem: The soul weeps," "Out of the Rains," "On Columbia Heights," and "In the Depths" previously appeared in *Mike & Dale's Younger Poets*, no. 9 (Spring 1998), pp. 2-5, 7, 9, eds. Michael Price and Dale Smith.

"Poem: To capture the feeling" previously appeared in *(Sic) Vice & Verse*, no. 1 (June 1998), p. 16, eds. Rafael F.J. Alvarado and S.A. Griffin.

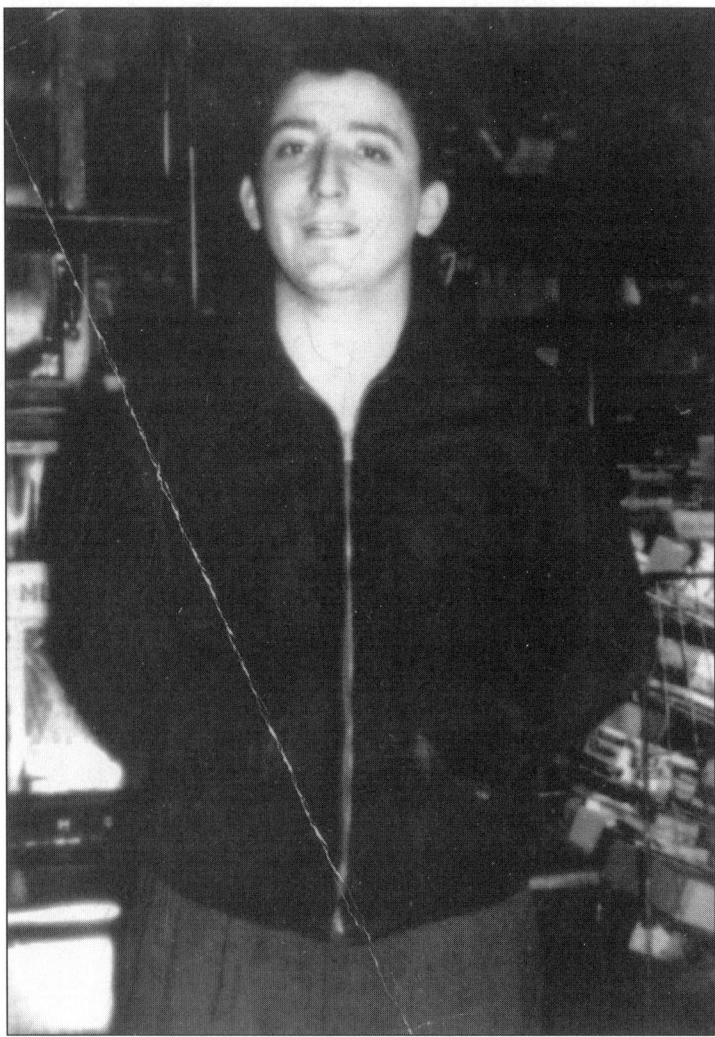

*Harvey Silver standing in a grocery store
in the Bronx, New York City, 1947.*

Reviews of Micheline Over the Years

"Micheline is a fine new poet, and that's something to crow about. He has that swinging free style I like...and [his] sweet lines revive the poetry of open hope in America."

— *Jack Kerouac*, 1958,
(introduction to RIVER OF RED WINE)

"It is as expected as it is generous that Mr. Kerouac would aid a lesser-known member of his Beat Generation to get an honest chance. So he has emerged from that hiding place he is so seldom in and written the introduction to the initial offering of The Troubador Poets, Jack Micheline's RIVER OF RED WINE AND OTHER POEMS.

"[T]here are good poems in RIVER OF RED WINE, powerful and filled with zest and sometimes touched with wild sorrow..."

— *Dorothy Parker*, Esquire, (September 1958), p. 12,
(reviewing RIVER OF RED WINE)

"a guy I like by god himself anyway even one little poem called 'My City': Jack Micheline; another nice thing abt him is how he comes on on [Hubert] Selby. He was here this week for a day and over (Micheline that is) and it was fine. He strikes me as the true later thing fr Jack [Kerouac] and Allen [Ginsberg] the genuine citizen beat—more than [Gregory] Corso who is literary and only substantively street. This Micheline is only life, and old-fashioned poet of same streets like forever jongleur."

— *Charles Olson*, letter to Robert Creeley,
July 31, 1960

"Dear Jack: What do you want your poems back for? They are good and I would like to keep them. But anybody who sends a stamped envelope deserves to get something back, I reckon. ... Poems I like most right now are JENNY LEE and OLD DOC and MOTHER so, before I send them all back, if you don't mind, tomorrow I'll copy those for myself."

— *Langston Hughes*, letter to Micheline,
October 20, 1960

"I get the same thrill of discovery from Jack Micheline's book as I had the first time I came upon Steinbeck's THE PASTURES OF HEAVEN and Saroyan's THE DARING YOUNG MAN ON THE FLYING TRAPEZE. Jack Micheline goes beyond the art of story-telling and brings us back to people. ...IN THE BRONX AND OTHER STORIES is a fine contribution to contemporary literature in general and especially to this country's marvellous history of innovation and exploration in poetry, which continues seemingly from nothing and out of nowhere as the madmen, like Jack Micheline, grow, develop and unfold. Through the irritating frustrations and silent rages of their personal lives so often neglected through the over-cautiousness of the literati, these poets still, somehow, quietly build and offer us monuments."

—*Kirby Congdon*, December 24, 1965,
(review accompanying notice of Micheline's reading at
The Folklore Center, January 24, 1966, New York City)

"There is within poetry a distinct tradition that is becoming obsolete. The tradition is the poet or the troubadour who goes about or wanders, roams over the country trading his songs and poems for bread and butter. It is from this tradition that Villon became prominent. Whitman too travelled West as recorded in Specimen Days and to New Orleans. One of the last poets in this tradition was Vachel Lindsay who took highly publicized walks and traded pamphlets, chapbooks for bread and food.

"There is only one poet who comes close to chronicling a similar lifestyle, trading his poems, songs and drawings for food, an urban street singer whose Basso Aspirante has been capturing audiences for the last twenty years and that poet is Jack Micheline."

—*Paul Mariah*, August 13, 1976,
(preface to **NORTH OF MANHATTAN**)

"Jack Micheline has genius for wino blues, down sad street blues, because he has an innate sense of rhythm and flashes of honesty under his stylization. J. Kerouac liked Micheline for his raw idealism and his ear, I think."

— *Allen Ginsberg*, postcard to Kristine Stiles,
August 24, 1976

"This is a book I would call an instant underground classic ... a sheaf of prose with the quality of Genet or Rechy... Slipped in the back jacket is a great recording of Micheline... All for $2.00. I'm glad to see these classics from North Beach. There are very few real ones left who have not been done in. And it is very difficult to maintain the real thing through strains of commerce ... some of its real substance can be found today in the works of Micheline, Pommy-Vega, Bob Kaufman and David Moe...

"It is a great little book, with a design of a rambler, one that should be passed along in dives and truckstops as a tearful salute. You have done it, Jack. You have pulled it off."

— *Charles Plymell*, book jacket praise which appeared on the photo offset copies of **Purple Submarine**, 1976

"Rebel that Micheline has been in the contemporary poetry scene, I would have pretty much suspected his work to take the turn with Rimbaud... a direct ascent into innovation, near obscurity. This is not the case. He has followed with chants, ballads, songs in the tradition of Villon rather than Rimbaud along with Whitman, Vachel Lindsay, Sandburg and Allen Ginsberg with a blues touch borrowed from Langston Hughes. To my mind, the poems in this collection share a more Blakean movement from 'songs of innocence' to 'songs of experience' gathered from the street scene... Read these haunting poems and grow."

—*Maurice Kenny*, "Jack Micheline Cruising Through Manhattan," *Contact II*, (Summer, 1978), pp. 19-20, (reviewing **NORTH OF MANHATTAN**)

"Poet and short-story writer Micheline is sometimes described as a precursor of Charles Bukowski, having been established in the latter's wild genre before Bukowski escaped from the post office."

—*Lawrence Ferlinghetti* and *Nancy J. Peters*, **LITERARY SAN FRANCISCO** (New York: Harper & Row, 1980)

"Jack Micheline is perhaps the best oral poet of his particular brand of poetry in America or abroad. Ferlinghetti won't read on the same bill if possible, and Ginsberg and his chants won't make it next to Mich either. At his best, he is the best! He captures an audience like no one else can...

"So you have the gentle Jack — silver-haired nomad Jew — and then you have the bad-mouthing Jack; the guy who throws up on your shoes at a reading or misses the bucket at Bukowski's home and wipes up the rotgut with one of Hank's manuscripts. He's lovable and a pain in the ass, but more than that; he's life at its best and worst; and how many people can you say that about? His heart is with the garbage collectors, dishwashers, factory workers, farm hands and bums, not with the academic gangsters who own the corporate trust of the universities. So Ginsberg, Corso, McClure, Ferlinghetti get the paid readings and Jack is ignored for being too rough, too loud, not playing the game the way it is supposed to be played."

—*A. D. Winans*, "Last of the Street Poets,"
Northeast Rising Sun, vol. 4, no. 18 (1980), pp. 22-23

"Among the rash of self-proclaimed and self-taught poets given prominence by the Beat Generation, Jack Micheline is one of the few who continued to produce vital poetry and to inspire younger writers throughout the two succeeding decades. A beloved friend and respected contemporary of such artists as James T. Farrell, William Saroyan, Franz Kline, and Charles Mingus, and the recipient of accolades from such fellow writers as Seymour Krim, Fielding Dawson, Charles Bukowski, and Andrei Voznesensky, Micheline has nevertheless remained "underground" and virtually unknown to the American critical and academic establishment."

— *Gerald Nicosia*, "Jack Micheline,"
DICTIONARY OF LITERARY BIOGRAPHY, VOLUME 16: THE BEATS: LITERARY BOHEMIANS IN POSTWAR AMERICA (Detroit, Michigan: Gale Research Co., 1983), p. 410

"Jack Micheline didn't have to struggle to not become a precious literary commodity. For all of his three and half decades as a poet he has lived outside of the universities and far from the parlors of conventional literature. His work, often thought of as too sentimental and untrained, comes right out of the tradition of American populist poetry that has always made the more cultivated and cultured feel a great deal less safe than what they generally find acceptable.

"Micheline is the street poet par excellance. He extols the poetry of Carl Sandburg, Vachel Lindsay and the little-known **AMERICAN ODES** of Sherwood Anderson. Rejecting the notion that a poetry must be finely attuned to avant garde trends and deeply schooled in past traditions, he has been a kind of wide open, American wordslinger, blaspheming anything that appears both false and comfortable and rejoicing in the lost souls and downtrodden people of good spirit and heart who he has met on his travels."

—Neeli Cherkovski, "Jack Micheline at the SF Press Club," *Haight Ashbury Literary Journal*, vol. 2, no. 2 (1986), p. 13

> Folks, read Jack Micheline,
>   n doubt about it
> He's a great poeit
> And see?—read Gregory Corso
>   too all about "bookies
>   & chickenpluckers"
> & Read Competition Ginsberg
>   the maddest brain
>   in poetry

—Jack Kerouac, from the 14th chorus of "Orlanda Blues" (written in 1957-58), **BOOK OF BLUES** (New York: Penguin Books, 1995)

"Of the practicing Beat poets — those that actually give readings in used bookstores, who can be found obnoxiously but eloquently drunk on street corners, that live in cheap hotels and sport a craggy look of unreconstructed defiance (to whatever it is you've got) — Jack Micheline keeps the jazzy faith best.

"At sixty-seven Jack Micheline remains the quintessential poet of the streets. His subject matter remains stinking hotels, racetracks, gamblers, bad teeth, evictions, whores and dreamers. His work has varied over the decades but his allegiance to the unsung has not."

> —*Victor Miller*, "The Poet of the Streets,"
> *New Mission News*, September 1997, p. 10
> (reviewing **Sixty-seven Poems for Downtrodden Saints**)

"It's been a terrible year for poets—Allen Ginsberg gone last spring, then William Burroughs, Denise Levertov, now Micheline.

"Jack was the equal of all of them. ... His bullhorn voice still fills the room, with anger and recalcitrance, with the jocular defiance of the have-nots of the world, the desperate, the beat, the illuminated, the crazed, the *maudits* of the world.

"Eugene Debbs (who said that while there was a soul in jail he was not free) would have loved him."

> —*Lawrence Ferlinghetti*, "Micheline, Micheline...,"
> *Nexus*, vol. 33, no. 3 (1998), p. 15

"Jack had the gift of moment. Called Whitman's wild child, he was also quite often, an almost unbearable pain in the ass, tolerated because he was sometimes capable of pulling daggers out of bleeding rock in the subterranean circus of hope. He had charm, had style. He liked the carnival wink of the con, the nickel/dime hustle, the broads, the bookies and the track and was captivated by the math of beating the odds; we call this seduction luck and try to rehearse it as if it could be owned. He could toss a good hand just to play the fool and was often drunk on bitter wine of his own terrible design yet witnessed the color all around him shouting, *"beauty is everywhere Baudelaire."*

"Jack Micheline was a poet."

> — *S.A. Griffin*, "Onword,"
> *Damaged Goods*, April/May 1998, p. 45

"Jack Micheline's voice rolls, builds, chants, scats; calls out the names of jazz like subway stops, makes baseball and dames and dirt roads and crushed dreams and uglybeautiful city streets carbon gone diamond. His poems are gut honest, delivered with a singular voice both powerful and tender..."

— *Laura Conway*, "Gaa Baby Gaa Onnnn,"
Optimism Monthly, Prague, No. 25, April 1998, p. 12

"Jack Micheline went the limit as a man and a poet, did not sell out and his poetry contains the joy and the anguish of his lifelong struggle to remain authentic to himself. May he serve as example to us all, and to future generations of poets."

— *Alan Kaufman*, posted on the internet at
www.jackmicheline.com, April 29, 1998

"Allen [Ginsberg] was finally what I thought was everywhere in the Village, a genuine book stuffed intellectual, and as well, a publicist, perhaps the best we knew of poetry itself. There were so many bullshitters and tasters and energetic dilettantes otherwise. Jammed in the coffee shops imitating Marlon Brando. Except Jack Micheline wasnt imitating, in those jazz poetry sessions he was who Marlon Brando was imitating."

— *Amiri Baraka*, "Blues for Allen,"
The Blacklisted Journalist, (e-zine), July 1, 1998, column 35

"I had the good fortune of meeting Jack Micheline and found him to be an officer and a gentleman. Also, he wrote poetry and the best of it sings."

— *Billy Childish*, letter to Matt Gonzalez,
August 18, 1998

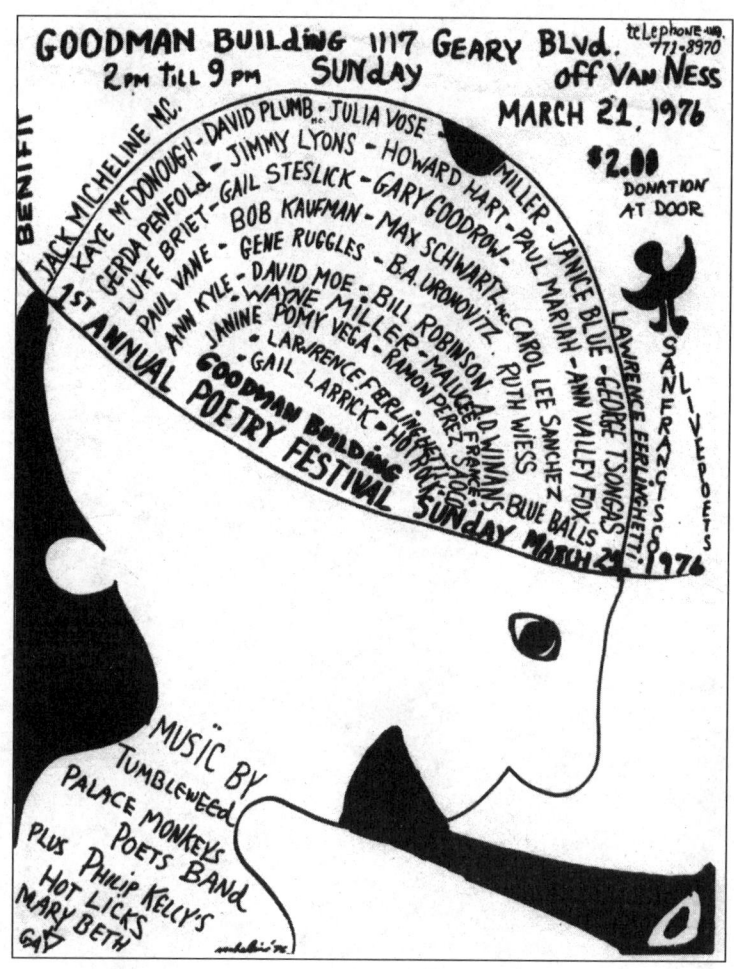

The flyer Micheline made to advertise the benefit reading held to save the 105 year old Goodman Building, home of many artists and poets, from demolition as part of an urban renewal plan in San Francisco, March 1976.

*Poem painting "One Arm for Ed Balchowsky," 1974.
Mixed media on paper, 24 3/4" x 18 1/4."
The text of this poem appears on page 109.*

Charles Bukowski on Micheline

"got your wild letter.... am I saying the wrong thing? it's Jan. 2, I think. 1968. the amatuer drunks have desisted. me, I missed work today, tough shit, they won't fire me because they torture me too much, it delights them.

"I have seen some of your stuff, Babe, and kind of like old Dosoevsky, wild dogs, warm beer, you got a powerful line, Babe, so don't quit the poem — jam it to them...

"...hearing from you makes your poems more real — flesh added to the paper, like.

"Fame and immortality are games for other people. If we're not recognized when we walk down the street, that's our luck. So long as the typer works the next time we sit down.

"My little girl likes me and that's plenty."
— *Charles Bukowski*, letter to Micheline,
January 2, 1968

"rumors on town hall reading of Bukowski, Corso, Micheline...impossible. didn't you know I have made it known for years that I don't read publicly?"
— *Charles Bukowski*, letter to Carl Weissner,
February 27, 1968

"hello Jack: after the bit with you, got drunk with Dan Georgakas and Darrel and their broads, just pulling together now. sorry I didn't pick you up on road but car couldn't stop without stalling — finally just made it into L.A., dead battery, running stop signs, going around corners, circling when red lights there, never stopping. a real wild ride, the scotch sweating out of my ears.

"Bryan holding a prose piece of yours plus some work.

space running out but either going to use your prose piece or another I have in mind. must go to OPEN CITY and check it out. also 3 or 4 other things hanging, things to do — beside — work the dead gig.

"it was a good visit with you, old boy. now to shave and leap into the monkey cage."

— *Charles Bukowski*, letter to Micheline,
August 6, 1968

"Write us some great rolling bellowing cat yowling cowboy beersong poems, Jack. You know how. Do it! Buk
"Tell us about the women and the buildings and the streets, and the sadness of the blood...."

— *Charles Bukowski*, undated note to Micheline
soliciting material for *Open City* magazine
in Los Angeles

"I led off with the Micheline poem last night. it really hooked them. I guess a number of the broads had known Jack. the whole reading was lucky and went quite well. of course, much at a reading depends upon how the reader feels. I felt fine last night and it worked."

— *Charles Bukowski*, letter to Jon and Louise Webb,
July 4, 1970

"Hello Jack: well, suck my tender typingass fingers, Brooklyn Jack's still alive and screaming... Yes, yes I'm still here, been bouncing between 2 women... you ain't been forgotten, man. Neeli and I, anyhow, talk about you often. and I wrote a couple of poems about you. ...one LOOKING FOR JACK MICHELENE.

"Your letter was a poem. I'll bet you pissed away that 5 grand superfecta $$$$ in 2 months. you're afraid of money, jack, and you're right, but, kid, we do need a little of it so we can have a place to sit down and type... I showed your letter to Linda and she laughed, "He's all right," she said, "sure, he's all right," I said."

— *Charles Bukowski*, letter to Micheline,
September 25, 1972

"Micheline was fine, god damn romantic hustler, he turned on high, he sings those lines, he's in rhythm and breaking through. he's half bullshit in person but that's just cover and bad nerves and too many nights in the cold alley. he knows he's got more than 90 percent of those who have broken through, and it hurts: Jack should have an agent. no publisher should ever see Jack. he's shell-shocked and tries to twist the arm. they resent it. but they're fools. the work is there. IN THE POEM. ...when Jack is turned on high he is capable of writing a better poem than I could ever write. I write more good poems over the long haul but when he is totally high and singing I can't touch him. if he stays at it and stops hounding the publishers and just does his work he will be found again long before he is dead."

—*Charles Bukowski*, letter to A. D. Winans,
January 21, 1974

"Hello Silver: got yor Dr. Freezein. thanks. it's a flowing josling(t) masterpiece you Jew drunk singer, very fine. you know best the betrayals, the pavements, the whores with lemon rinds up their bungs and the lice in the spotlights. things like that."

—*Charles Bukowski*, letter to Micheline,
August 1975

"Miche[line] has never got his just due but it's as well — it'll keep him on his spring instead of turning him into a silky-haired, over-read, over-precious N. Mailer. overexposure is the toughest whore of all. and one that few men can turn away for a head job."

—*Charles Bukowski*, letter to A. D. Winans,
November 30, 1976

"Hey Jack — you got any rich friends? See enclosed circ. Hand to them. Been fucked-up drinking. Still hanging to job that is killing me. Health worse and worse. I assassinate myself because there are no people. I must learn to live with ants, fish, spiders...

"You got a poem manuscript or batch of poems??? Send c/o John Martin, c/o Black Sparrow Press. Tell him Bukowski sent you. Royalties not bad, depending upon # copies printed. Worth a try, I'd think, but up to you."

—*Charles Bukowski*, undated letter to Micheline

"Jack Micheline by a couple of nights ago. he talked and drank and read me his poems and showed me his drawings, then slept on the couch and pewked all over the place, missing the huge wastebasket I had placed right where his head was supposed to be."

—*Charles Bukowski*, letter to Carl Weissner,
July 16, 1978

Cover of Micheline's book, **Last House in America**, edited by A.D. Winans and published by Second Coming Press in San Francisco in 1976, in an edition of 500 copies. The cover photo is by Bil Paul.

Concerning the "Skinny Dynamite" Obscenity Case

"Last Monday, [John] Bryan was arraigned on charges stemming from publication of an article by Beat Poet Jack Micheline in *Open City* some time ago. Stanley Fleischman, one of the country's leading First Amendment attorneys and former member of the ACLU board of directors, has been retained to handle the case. To raise funds to cover legal expenses for this second arrest, Bryan is conducting a benefit Sunday at Cinematheque 16 in Pasadena. His arrest Oct. 30 by a Sheriff's vice squad deputy arose over the publication [of] a poem called "Skinny Dynamite" — a prose description of a girl in Brooklyn who likes to fuck, Bryan said. In the complaint, sheriff's vice officer, Deputy Donald Sivard, said that after reading the story, it was of his opinion that 'it was without any socially redeeming importance.'"

—*Julie Russo*, "John Bryan appeal,"
Los Angeles Free Press, (November 8-13, 1968), p. 3

"I have been acquainted with Jack Micheline's writing for approximately ten years and have admired his very real ability both to celebrate and lament the wonders of our ordinary lives. In doing this he has often reawakened and enlarged my own sympathy for my fellow beings, which I feel is one of the good things a good poet should do for us. Certainly the story 'Skinny Dynamite' aims for the same sympathetic awakening. I am in fact stunned that at this point in our cultural development there should be any question at all about obscenity in relation to this story. To have to discuss it in those terms is to return to a situation from the past, when it was impossible to speak publicly and freely about the total reality of our lives. The integrity of Mr.

Micheline's work should need no such defense in the year 1968. I will, therefore, not insult that work by pretending to defend it, but will only register my belief that he has succeeded as an artist in making us aware of one aspect of man's often desperate condition in this world. He has done this in a style that shows a great care for depiction, and with a purity of language responsive to its source that deserves our admiration."

— *Jerome Rothenberg*, letter to Stanley Fleischman, December 10, 1968

"I understand that John Bryan and his *Open City* newspaper have gotten into difficulties over a story called 'Skinny Dynamite' by Jack Micheline. Micheline is a creative writer. I believe him to be very sincere, very talented, and if he does offend some elements of society, I would rather alter those elements than change a single word of Micheline's writing. In the case of his 'Skinny Dynamite' short story; it seems obvious to me that such situations as Micheline graphically describes do in fact exist, and publishers such as John Bryan have the responsibility to bring the fact of their existence to the public attention, rather than ignore them in the false name of decency."

— *Stephen Schneck*, letter to Stanley Fleischman, December 23, 1968

"I have read 'Skinny Dynamite' and am quite amazed that a man should be arrested for publishing this story. I can understand why some people may be upset by suddenly having an aspect of reality thrust in their face, but that certainly does not constitute a crime. Obviously there are scenes and language in the story that might offend certain people, but to accuse a man of being a criminal for publishing a story that is an artistic reflection of the truth is, in itself, a crime. There are certain truths we would all like to hide from, but a man is not a criminal for forcing us to become aware of them, no matter how much they may scare us."

— *Hubert Selby, Jr.*, statement accompanying letter to Stanley Fleischman, February 5, 1969

"Mr. Micheline and I have had many conversations regarding literary style for over a decade, and I was pleased to see that the text of 'Skinny Dynamite' shows him perfecting a lesson in composition taught to all American writers by the late eminent poet-doctor William Carlos Williams, that is, a precise eye and an economical phrasing for concrete particular details of persons, looks, scenes, situations and actions."

— *Allen Ginsberg*, letter to Stanley Fleischman, February 23, 1969

"'Skinny Dynamite' is a story which presents obvious problems to anyone who wishes to publish it, but I believe it has literary merit. It is comparable to a story called "Tra-la-la" in LAST EXIT TO BROOKLYN (Grove Press), whose language was equally explicit; but 'Skinny Dynamite' has its own lyrical intensity. I am not a believer in the principle of defending all sexual writing as non-pornographic, no matter what its content, intent, or execution. But 'Skinny Dynamite' is, in my opinion, literature, for it seeks to deal, and I think deals successfully, with the completeness of experience in what society is sometimes fond to call its social depths, and so it rises from being a document to being a short affirmative work of prose."

— *Norman Mailer*, statement prepared for Stanley Fleischman, 1969

THIRD RAIL (2)

35 cents. U. S.
4 pesos

The Land of the Savage

America is a savage land. Having the first time in many years the opportunity to leave my native land. I am able to look at it with a sense of a free mind not being in the middle of things. What does it mean to be human? That is the first question I want to bring up. In America everybody is running around trying to be, or prove something to someone else. The ability to communicate on a human level has almost completely disappeared. The ability to love and extend oneself without fear has almost diminished. The feeling that one must be first, that one must be ahead of the other is also a falicy. There is no chance to breathe. So people race like dogs in a blind strecth of darkness going nowhere, and burning out there energy. In America the material things seem first to the mass mind. The greed to possess things have taken away from the human values. The greed for profit first has made our country a huge market place of a low human form. The dignity of the human being lie crouched in a pit of fear and madness. One is brought up like a machine and human love from what springs the s o u r c e of all beautiful things always secondary. In the Universities and Colleges the student minds are taken away and they become fodder and flunkies in the big corporations. Almost nowhere is the individual encouraged to think for himself, to believe in his inner beliefs. The Universities have become a machine of destruction of the individual mind. We have become a nation of dissolution, a nation a disbelief. And where is the rebellion and dissent of the young? We must inspire the young and bring back dignity to the human being. America is land of fear. It is an i n h u m a n and fearfull land. It is the l a n d of the s a v a g e . We are a f r a i d to look at ourselves in any true light. We are second class because of our denial of human values, are inability to extend ourselves as human beings and the fear of honest relationships between one another. We have become a pretentious and untruthfull land. It is a land that looks good from the outside, and within it is full of cancer and death. Its real true voices are very rarely heard. It is a land with the greatest m e n t a l sickness in the world. It is a land of the outside apperance. The land of the prop. In America we export Marilyn Monroe and her physical beauty will be shown on the screens of the world. Yet what lies within the pain and torture of this woman. Above all America is ashamed to be human. We are afraid to look at ourselves in any t r u e

(2)